The Funniest People in Music: 250 Anecdotes

David Bruce

Published by David Bruce, 2022.

THE FUNNIEST PEOPLE IN MUSIC: 250 ANECDOTES

First edition. September 14, 2022.

ISBN: 979-8215681633

Written by David Bruce.

Table of Contents

Dedication

Dedicated to Carl Eugene Bruce and Josephine Saturday Bruce

My father, Carl Eugene Bruce, died on 24 October 2013. He used to work for Ohio Power, and at one time, his job was to shut off the electricity of people who had not paid their bills. He sometimes would find a home with an impoverished mother and some children. Instead of shutting off their electricity, he would tell the mother that she needed to pay her bill or soon her electricity would be shut off. He would write on a form that no one was home when he stopped by because if no one was home he did not have to shut off their electricity.

The best good deed that anyone ever did for my father occurred after a storm that knocked down many power lines. He and other linemen worked long hours and got wet and cold. Their feet were freezing because water got into their boots and soaked their socks. Fortunately, a kind woman gave my father and the other linemen dry socks to wear.

My mother, Josephine Saturday Bruce, died on 14 June 2003. She used to work at a store that sold clothing. One day, an impoverished mother with a baby clothed in rags walked into the store and started shoplifting in an interesting way: The mother took the rags off her baby and dressed the infant in new clothing. My mother knew that this mother could not afford to buy the clothing, but she helped the mother dress her baby and then she watched as the mother walked out of the store without paying.

***

The doing of good deeds is important. As a free person, you can choose to live your life as a good person or as a bad person. To be a good person, do good deeds. To be a bad person, do bad deeds. If you do good deeds, you will become good. If you do bad deeds, you will become bad. To become the person you want to be, act as if you already are that kind of person. Each of us chooses what kind of person we will become. To become a good person, do the things a good person does. To become a bad person, do the things a bad person does. The opportunity to take action to become the kind of person you want to be is yours.

Human beings have free will. According to the Babylonian Niddah 16b, whenever a baby is to be conceived, the Lailah (angel in charge of contraception) takes the drop of semen that will result in the conception and asks God, "Sovereign of the Universe, what is going to be the fate of this drop? Will it develop into a robust or into a weak person? An intelligent or a stupid person? A wealthy or a poor person?" The Lailah asks all these questions, but it does not ask, "Will it develop into a righteous or a wicked person?" The answer to that question lies in the decisions to be freely made by the human being that is the result of the conception.

A Buddhist monk visiting a class wrote this on the chalkboard: "EVERYONE WANTS TO SAVE THE WORLD, BUT NO ONE WANTS TO HELP MOM DO THE DISHES." The students laughed, but the monk then said, "Statistically, it's highly unlikely that any of you will ever have the opportunity to run into a burning orphanage and rescue an infant. But, in the smallest gesture of kindness — a warm smile, holding the door for the person behind you, shoveling the driveway of the elderly person next door — you have committed an act of immeasurable profundity, because to each of us, our life is our universe."

In her book titled *I Have Chosen to Stay and Fight*, comedian Margaret Cho writes, "I believe that we get complimentary snack-size portions of the afterlife, and we all receive them in a different way." For Ms. Cho, many of her snack-size portions of the afterlife come in hip hop music. Other people get different snack-size portions of the afterlife, and we all must be on the lookout for them when they come our way. And perhaps doing good deeds and experiencing good deeds are snack-size portions of the afterlife.

Cover Illustration for *The Funniest People in Music:* Caitlin Kraus

Caitlin Kraus, who created the self-portrait for a flyer advertising her concert, wrote, "I've only actually got five fingers on each hand... just didn't want to disappoint anyone if that's what would entice you to come out. I don't use AI usually since real art is my thing, but I always make these flyers on Canva myself anyway, so thought I'd have a little fun."

Caitlin Kraus (she/her), LPCC, MT-BC

Licensed Professional Clinical Counselor

Music Therapist - Board Certified

Ohio University Counseling & Psych Services

www.ohio.edu/counseling

Follow OU Counseling & Psych Services on Twitter at @OHIO_Counseling

CAITLIN KRAUS ON FACEBOOK

https://www.facebook.com/caitlinkrausmusic

CAITLIN KRAUS MUSIC

https://caitlinkrausmusic.com

CAITLIN KRAUS ON INSTAGRAM

https://www.instagram.com/caitlinkrausmusic/

CAITLIN KRAUS ON BANDCAMP

https://caitlinkrausmusic.bandcamp.com

CAITLIN KRAUS ON SPOTIFY

https://open.spotify.com/artist/7G2SiE8RWYUMZWLX1iGLPz?autoplay=true

CAITLIN KRAUS ON YOUTUBE MUSIC

https://music.youtube.com/channel/UCWt9a1zAjicyED4CuT-PEXw

***

All anecdotes have been retold in my own words to avoid plagiarism.

Anecdotes are usually short humorous stories. Sometimes they are thought-provoking or informative, not amusing.

Do you know a language other than English? If you do, I give you permission to translate this book, copyright your translation, publish or self-publish it, and keep all the royalties for yourself. (Do give me credit, of course, for the original book.)

Chapter 1: From Activism to Christmas

Activism

• Jazz musician Duke Ellington was active in the civil rights movement. In Baltimore, he performed at a concert. Afterward, he presented himself at a restaurant where African-American students had protested segregation. Like the students, Mr. Ellington was not permitted to eat at the restaurant, but his action succeeded in giving lots of publicity to the civil rights struggle in Baltimore. In addition, Mr. Ellington declined to perform a concert in Little Rock, Arkansas, after learning that the audience would be segregated. A short time later, he did perform in Dallas and Houston — but only after he was promised that blacks and whites in the audience could sit together.[1]

• Because African-American actor/singer Paul Robeson used his right of free speech to criticize prejudice and injustice in USAmerica, the United States government revoked his passport. In 1952, he attempted to cross the border into Canada — which was normally permitted even when one didn't have a passport — but he was stopped at the border. It looked as if the concert he had planned to give to benefit Canadian union workers would have to be cancelled, but the workers traveled to the border, and Mr. Robeson sang to them from across the border in the United States.[2]

• World-famous cellist Pablo Casals often took a stand for his beliefs. In Brussels, Belgium, he once declined to perform unless the musicians were paid for their rehearsal time. Tickets had been sold to the rehearsals, and Mr. Casals believed that the musicians ought to be paid when they performed at any event that people paid to attend. In addition, when Francisco Franco took control of Spain, Mr. Casals opposed him, and he declined to perform in countries that recognized Francisco Franco's fascist government.[3]

• On a trip to Southern Rhodesia, which was then part of the British empire but is now the self-ruled country of Zimbabwe, jazz musician Louis Armstrong insisted that he play only in front of integrated audiences. For the opening concert, 25,000 people showed up and the seats were filled with both blacks and whites. During his concert, Mr. Armstrong looked out over the audience and said, "I gotta tell y'all something — it's very nice to see this."[4]

• Pianist Artur Rubinstein cancelled a tour in Italy because of the then-government's anti-Semitism; he also returned a prestigious award — the Order of the Commander of the Crown. Although people talked about how much money Mr. Rubinstein would lose, he talked about how many hearts he would win. He signed the letter with which he returned the award, "Artur Rubinstein, Jewish pianist."[5]

• World-renowned conductor Pierre Monteux was once denied a room at a hotel, but when the manager discovered that Mr. Monteux was famous, he said that he could arrange a room for him because Mr. Monteux was "somebody." Mr. Monteux refused the room and departed, saying, "Everybody is somebody."[6]

Age

• The aged conductor Serge Koussevitsky disliked the spiritless playing of a musician, so he told him, "Don't play like an old man." The musician responded, "You are an old man yourself." Maestro Koussevitsky replied, "I know that. But when I conduct like an old man, I will give up the job." The musician thereafter played with spirit. [7]

• For decades, Sir Thomas Beecham conducted from memory. However, in his old age he sometimes used a score while conducting. When Neville Cardus asked him about this, Sir Thomas replied, "I have been going through my scores recently, and I find that they hold my interest from the first page to the last."[8]

• Latin singer Ricky Martin, famous especially for the huge hit "Livin' *la Vida Loca*" ("Living the Crazy Life"), sang when he was a teenager as a member of the Latin boy band Menudo, but he left the group before he turned 18. He had to — the group's mandatory retirement age was 17. (Some sources say age 16.)[9]

Alcohol

• During the early part of the 20th century, dancer Anna Pavlova toured in Milwaukee, Wisconsin, which is famous for its beer. There, Ms. Pavlova's music director, Theodore Stier, asked a traffic officer where he could find a place in Milwaukee that sold really good German beer. The traffic officer looked Mr. Stier over for a moment, and then he said, "Brother, there's a place on every block — thank God!"[10]

• Shortly after Edwin McArthur had become the accompanist for soprano Kirsten Flagstad, he struggled as he attempted to open a champagne bottle in her dressing room. She watched him for a moment and then told him, "Here, Edwin — this is more important for you to learn than all the songs we will do together." She then taught him how to open a champagne bottle.[11]

Animals

• While overseas entertaining troops in the Middle East during the Second World War, Joyce Grenfell was singing when a mouse ran over her foot. Because she was occupied, she didn't even notice the mouse, but her accompanist did — and played the rest of the concert without using the piano's pedals because she kept her feet off the floor. While in the Middle East, they were warned to shake out their shoes each morning before putting them on in case snakes or scorpions were curled up inside.[12]

• In Giuseppe Verdi's opera *Rigoletto* is a scene in which the title character throws into a river a sack containing what is supposed to be the dead body of his enemy. Unfortunately, at a 1950 performance at Sadler's Wells Theatre in London, a kitten wandered on stage during the scene and was fascinated with the sack. The kitten kept digging its claws into the sack, and the "dead body" inside the sack kept squirming. Finally, the singer playing Rigoletto noticed the kitten and removed it from the stage.[13]

• Katheryn Bloodgood, a mezzo-soprano, was singing at Oberlin College in Oberlin, Ohio, when a bat flew into the recital hall. While she was finishing singing a Henschel lullaby that was supposed to end with the word *"shu"* sung very quietly, the bat flew directly at her. Instead of singing *"shu"* very quietly, she shrieked the word and then ran offstage to escape from the bat.[14]

• During a New Orleans production of the opera *Nabucco*, a horse committed a large indiscretion on stage. The producer, Jim Lucas, ordered the stagehands to clean up the mess, only to find out that they didn't have a shovel. Angrily, he shouted, "Don't you know you never hire a horse without a shovel?"[15]

• The conductor Artur Nikisch was very popular and received many letters from women who asked him for a lock of his hair. A friend told him that he would soon go bald because he always responded to these letters. Mr. Nikisch smiled and then said, "I won't go bald — but my dog might."[16]

• Tenor Gilbert Louis Duprez once sang a high C in Gioacchino Rossini's apartment. Mr. Rossini checked to see if any of his glassware had shattered; later, he said that the tone of the high C had been like "the squawk of a capon whose throat is being cut."[17]

Audiences

• In Vienna, Alfred Piccaver and Elizabeth Schumann gave a joint recital, the program of which promised that they would sing a duet from *La Boheme*. Unfortunately, the pianist brought the wrong music, so they sang a duet from *Madama Butterfly* instead. Nevertheless, the audience declined to go home until they had heard the *Boheme* duet, so the house manager asked the audience, "Is there a *Boheme* [score] in the house?" A person in the gallery answered, "I've got one." Borrowing the score, the pianist played the duet and the audience was able to hear Mr. Piccaver and Ms. Schumann sing it.[18]

• Leopold Stokowski, conductor of the Philadelphia Orchestra, was so distressed by the lack of manners displayed by audiences that he decided to do something about it. At a concert, he had many musicians arrive late and noisily make their way to their seats. He also had some musicians talk noisily throughout the concert. Finally, he had some of the musicians leave the concert in a hurry a few minutes before the performance was finished. The audience laughed at the actions of the musicians, but the audience continued to act the same way it had been acting.[19]

• Celebrities are adored everywhere, but are they adored for their talents or for the hype surrounding them? Enrico Caruso — a gifted tenor — once decided to find out. During a performance of Leoncavallo's *Pagliacci*, he stood off stage and sang Beppe's Act II serenade. Had he been onstage, he would have caused a sensation, but after he had sung out of the sight of the audience (without his presence having been announced), no one applauded his singing.[20]

• Sir Rudolf Bing enjoyed telling the story of an incompetent tenor from Chemnitz who went to Bremen for an audition. Although the tenor was terrible, many people in the audience applauded and shouted such encouragement as "Wonderful! Wonderful! Stay here! Stay here!" Why? Because many of the members of the audience were from Chemnitz.[21]

• Hans von Bülow once played piano in front of a very appreciative audience, and even after he had played several encores, the audience showed no signs of going home. Therefore, Von Bülow threatened, "If you don't stop this applause, I will play all of Bach's 48 preludes and fugues, from beginning to end!" The threat worked, and the audience went home.[22]

• Audiences tend to like happy endings. Gioacchino Rossini wrote the opera *Otello*, based of course on William Shakespeare's *Othello*, but the audience hated the ending, and kept trying to warn Desdemona that Othello was going to murder her. Eventually, Rossini was forced to change the ending to a happy one where Othello and Desdemona reconcile.[23]

• In 1949, before Victoria de los Angeles had become a famous soprano, she traveled to Oslo for two concerts. At the first concert, barely 30 people attended. However, news of good singers travels fast. At the second concert only two days later, over 1,000 people tried to attend the concert but couldn't because the concert hall was full.[24]

Auditions

• James Morris' voice teacher, Nicola Moscona, helped him greatly during his audition with the Metropolitan Opera. On the morning of the audition, Mr. Morris was understandably nervous, and he vomited. He telephoned Mr. Moscona, who took him — and a bag — to the Met. During the audition, Mr. Morris sang one aria, but when he was asked to sing another, his mind went blank. Fortunately, Mr. Moscona hissed at him, "*Simone, stupido, Simone.*" Mr. Morris sang the *Simone Boccanegra* bass aria and the Met offered him a contract.[25]

• Early in her career, Moravian soprano Maria Jeritza auditioned for the director of the Vienna Volksoper, Rainer Simons. Halfway through her first song, Micaeli's aria from *Carmen*, he shouted, "Stop! That's enough!" Ms. Jeritza complained that he hadn't allowed her to finish even one song, but he explained, "I didn't need any more — I'm engaging you."[26]

Autographs

• The great Norwegian soprano Kirsten Flagstad used to enjoy giving autographs to fans who wrote to her for them, but she was surprised when several fans complained that the autographs weren't genuine, but were instead written by her secretary. After investigating, she discovered what the problem was. Not only did Ms. Flagstad write the autograph, but she also wrote the names and addresses on the envelopes she used to send her autograph to her fans. Fans compared the writing, noticed that it was done by the same hand, and incorrectly concluded that a secretary had written the autographs.[27]

• Irish tenor John McCormack adored Italian tenor Enrico Caruso, and early in his career he bought a photograph of Mr. Caruso and forged on it an inscription from Mr. Caruso to himself. Later, he met Mr. Caruso and told him about the forgery. Amused, Mr. Caruso produced another photograph of himself and wrote this real inscription on it: "To McCormack, very friendly, Enrico Caruso."[28]

Awards

• As a teenager, Ella Fitzgerald lived on the streets of Harlem. One day, although she was wearing ragged clothing and had gone without a bath for weeks, she entered a talent contest at the Apollo Theater. The audience loved her, and she won first place, but she never received her prize. The prize was the opportunity to sing at the Apollo Theater for a week, but theater management thought that Ella was too physically dirty to be an entertainer. Soon afterward, Ella became recognized as a great jazz vocalist.[29]

• The theme song of the United States Navy is "Anchors Aweigh," whose music was composed by Navy Academy bandmaster Charles A. Zimmerman. Every year, bandmaster Zimmerman was given a medal by the graduating class in recognition of the excellence of "Anchors Aweigh." According to the official Annapolis history, because of his many medals bandmaster Zimmerman would have drowned instantly if he had ever fallen overboard.[30]

Bathrooms

• Singing at outdoor concerts while wearing fabulous, elegant gowns does have a downside. In 1995, at Radley College, soprano Leslie Garrett discovered that her dress, because of its width, would not permit her to use a portaloo (in America, the term is "portapotty"). For the first half of the concert, she sang with her legs crossed. In the meantime, the concert organizers set up a tent, complete with a bucket, for her use during the interval (in the USA, the term is "intermission"). [31]

• Famous violinist Szymon Goldberg had some unusual talents. Once, he was disturbed during a concert by some background noise, so he stopped playing and requested a wrench. He went backstage, fixed a continuously running toilet, and then resumed playing.[32]

Big Breaks

• Movie clichés sometimes come to life. Opera singer Mary Garden started her career at the top. She was in Paris studying singing, and she attended an Opera-Comique rehearsal of *Louise* and fell in love with it. She acquired a copy of the score, and began studying it intensively. She attended performances of the opera, and she took notes on where the singers stood on stage and all the details of acting she could jot down. On Friday, April 13, 1900, she received a note telling her to go to the Opéra-Comique, where she received the news that the woman who regularly sang the title role of *Louise* was ill and might not be able to perform, and so she was given a ticket and asked to sit in the audience that night just in case she were needed. Act 1 passed well, as the title character sang little in it, but during the intermission the star singer rushed out of the opera house. Ms. Garden took her place, made a huge hit, and signed a well-paying contract at the Opéra-Comique.[33]

• Buffy Sainte-Marie became a professional folk musician by accident. She had learned to play a second-hand guitar as a child, and in 1963, during a visit to New York City, she sang and played for fun at a coffeehouse in Greenwich Village. A music critic for *The New York Times* happened to be in the audience, and he gave her a glowing review. Soon she was performing concerts and making records. Despite her long-term success, Ms. Sainte-Marie says, "I never expected to last more than a year or two."[34]

Chamber Music

• Not everyone likes chamber music. Arthur Catterall used to lead the BBC Symphony. One day, he was in a taxi when the driver looked at his violin and asked if he ever played on the radio. When Mr. Catterall replied that he did, the cabbie asked, "Do you ever take part in those Sunday afternoons of chamber music?" Mr. Catterall replied in the affirmative, so the cabbie stopped his taxi, opened the door, and said, "Well, you can jolly well walk!"[35]

• Chamber music can be very expensive. Thomas Beecham spent much of his own money on music. Once, a gentleman from the United States who had been donating much money to an orchestra compared notes with him. After their talk, the American gentleman said, "Well, sir, I guess that every time some guy draws a bow across a fiddle, you or I sign a check for a thousand dollars."[36]

Children

• When he was an old man, Sir Thomas Beecham conducted a Sir Robert Mayer Children's Concert. He slowly walked to the conductor's chair, and then spoke to the audience of children, saying, "Ladies and gentlemen, my slow progress to the conductor's desk was due not to any reluctance on my part to conduct before so distinguished an audience. My slow progress was due entirely to the infirmity of old age. Our first piece is by Mozart. It was composed when he was at the age of …" — here Sir Thomas pointed to a small boy in the audience — "at your age, sir."[37]

• As a very young child, soprano Geraldine Farrar started taking piano lessons, but she played only the black keys. Asked why she didn't play the white keys, she replied, "Because the white keys seem like angels and the black keys like devils, and I like devils best." In an early autobiography, she wrote, "It was the soft half-tones of the black keys which fascinated me, and to this day I prefer their sensuous harmony to that of the more brilliant 'angels.'"[38]

• When English entertainer Joyce Grenfell was a young girl, her father took her to hear some Bach at the Victoria and Albert Museum. She tried to beat time with the music with her head, but was unable to — the boy in the seat behind her had fallen asleep and his knees had trapped her ponytail! Because she was polite, she waited until the music had ended and the applause had wakened the boy, who freed her ponytail.[39]

• In 1909, when tenor Leo Slezak sang the part of Tamino in Mozart's *Magic Flute* at the Metropolitan Opera, Walter, his little son, was in the audience. Little Walter had been told the plot of the opera, and he knew that a snake would be chasing Tamino at his entrance. Out of excitement, when little Walter saw his father make his entrance, he shouted, "Watch out, Papa! There is a snake!"[40]

• At age 13, Billie Holiday went to New York City to be rejoined with her mother, but she took a walk in Harlem and got lost. A social worker helped her out by finding her a place to stay until her mother could be located — a place that young Billie remembered as a beautiful hotel. After she grew up, Ms. Holiday went back to the "beautiful hotel" and discovered that it was a YWCA.[41]

• One mother thought that her three-year-old daughter might be a musical genius because the little girl remembered where the middle C key was located on the piano keyboard after being shown it once. However, one day the mother cleaned the piano keys, and her little daughter couldn't pick out middle C anymore — the middle C key had been the one with the egg stain.[42]

• As a concert pianist, Denis Matthews had to practice long and hard. Following breakfast one day, he went to his music room and began practicing the Brahms B flat Concerto. Several hours later, when it was his young daughter's bedtime, he was still practicing. As she was saying good night to her father, she said, "If ever I do music when I grow up, I'm going to do it for FUN!"[43]

• Elizabeth Soderstrom brought her children to see her in the opera *The Mines of Sulphur*. Her two oldest children loved it — especially the part when her character opened her cloak to show the spots that indicated that she had the plague. Unfortunately, her youngest child was terrified and for a few weeks kept looking at people to see if they had spots.[44]

• When he was 11 years old, Leonard Bernstein started taking piano lessons. He immediately loved the piano, and sometimes early in the morning, he would get out of bed and play. His father once told him, "Lenny, don't you know it's two o'clock?" Young Leonard replied, "I know. But the sounds are in my head and I just have to get them out." [45]

• Fritz, the brother of lieder singer Lotte Lehmann, was a terror when he and she were young, although he became very supportive of her and her career when they grew up. As a young boy, he used to pretend to be an Indian, kidnap her dolls, scalp them, paint the roots of the dolls' hair red, and hang them dripping from his belt.[46]

• As a young girl, comedian Beatrice Lillie got one of her first laughs while in church. She was singing in a choir, when a woman beside her passed gas loudly during a pause in the music. Young Beatrice turned to the woman and said, "Well, really!"[47]

• Entertainer Terri Balash, a star of *Godspell*, enjoyed performing even as a youngster. When she was six years old, she sometimes walked into her parents' parties and announced, "Okay, I'm going to entertain now, so everybody listen."[48]

Christmas

• When in grade school, future lieder singer Lotte Lehmann was insulted when one of her compositions was returned to her marked, "Judging from the accomplishments hitherto displayed in school, I doubt the authenticity of this work." In other words, her teacher thought young Lotte was plagiarizing because the quality of the composition was so good. Therefore, young Lotte demanded that she be allowed to write another composition as the teacher watched her to make sure she was not plagiarizing. Her teacher told her to write about Christmas, she did so as he watched her, and she proved that she was capable of writing good, original compositions.[49]

• Near Christmas, the Music Department of Colorado College in Colorado Springs performed Handel's *Messiah*, which was simulcast on the radio by station KKTV. The radio announcer was daydreaming when he suddenly realized that *The Messiah* was coming to an end, and he needed to play a record — quickly. He grabbed the first record he came across and put it on a turntable. The radio audience heard the end of *The Messiah*, the announcer identifying the station, and then a record playing "Happy Birthday to You."[50]

Chapter 2: From Clothing to Fans

Clothing

• When he was a child, singer James Brown's family was impoverished, and he was frequently sent home from school because his clothing was in such poor shape. In fact, one reason he began stealing was so he could have decent clothing. Of course, the stealing eventually led to his arrest. After being found guilty of stealing a car battery, he was sentenced to 8 to 16 years in prison.[51]

• Pop singer Madonna was an original even as a schoolgirl. Like the other students, Madonna wore a uniform at school, but she kept her school locker stocked with colorful hair bows and socks so she could be different from her classmates.[52]

Comedians

• Will Rogers seldom hurt anyone with his jokes. However, in his vaudeville days, he once was preceded by a singing act called the Cherry Sisters. During his act, he said that they must have decided on their name before they learned about lemons. After making the joke, Will realized that it was hurtful, so he apologized to the Cherry Sisters.[53]

• Jack Benny was not a virtuoso violinist, but neither was he as bad as he pretended to be to get laughs. After Mr. Benny played the violin well at a benefit, a friend said, "Jack, I didn't know you played the violin so beautifully." Mr. Benny replied, "When I was younger, they used to call me another Heifetz. Not Jascha — *another* Heifetz."[54]

Composers

• As a young boy, pianist Carl Czerny heard a family friend named Gelinek talk about how he was looking forward to meeting a pianist later that night at a party and how he and his friends were going to "thrash him" in a piano competition. The next day, however, Gelinek had to admit that he had been defeated: "That young man is possessed of the devil. Never have I heard such playing! He improvised on a theme I proposed like I never heard even Mozart improvise. Then he played compositions of his own, which are wonderful and grandiose to the highest degree." Czerny's father asked about the rival pianist's name. "He is a short, ugly, swarthy, and obstinate-looking young man," Gelinek replied, "and his name is Beethoven."[55]

• Composer Igor Stravinsky loved to have a good time with his friends. On his 80th birthday, several people threw parties for him — one person invited him over for cocktails, another person invited him over for dinner, and so on. When all the little parties were over, he said, "Well, that was marvelous. Thank you very much. I'm going home." The other people said, "Very well," so he asked, "Isn't anyone else going home?" They said no, for they were going out again to get drinks and perhaps do some dancing. Mr. Stravinsky then said, "What? You think that I'm going home to bed when all the rest of you are going out on the town?"[56]

• George Frideric Handel composed the *Messiah*, well known for its "Hallelujah" chorus. During a rehearsal for its premiere in Dublin, he became angry at a man named Janson, who was one of the bassos. "I thought you told me that you could read music at sight," complained Handel. "I can," Janson replied, "but not at first sight."[57]

• Gioacchino Rossini was giving singing lessons to a girl whose sister asked him, "Why don't you write any new music?" He replied, "A waste of time, my dear girl. It's impossible for the singers to perform what I've already written."[58]

Conductors

• Meredith Willson, author of *The Music Man*, had a great respect for Arturo Toscanini, who was an invited guest at the symphony orchestra where Mr. Willson worked. While the orchestra was practicing a dissonant symphonic poem named *"Feste Romane"* by Ottorino Respighi, Maestro Toscanini stopped the orchestra and told Mr. Gerhardt, a clarinet player, "F sharp, F sharp, F sharp." This happened five or six times, with Mr. Gerhardt protesting to Mr.

Willson (no one protests to Maestro Toscanini!), "I *am* playing F sharp. I've been playing it since the beginning." At this time, the clarinet player unconsciously — clarinet players do this occasionally by habit — held his instrument horizontally and blew some water out from under some of the very small keys. Once again, the orchestra launched into the piece and at its end, Maestro Toscanini said, "At last F sharp — *grazie a Dio*!" According to Mr. Willson, the water under the key had caused the note to sound F natural — and Maestro Toscanini heard the incorrect note through all the dissonance of the musical composition although the man who had actually played the note could not hear that it was incorrect![59]

• When he was young, Clemens Kraus was asked to be a guest conductor of the Vienna Philharmonic Orchestra, which the composer Johannes Brahms himself used to conduct. At the rehearsal of a Brahms symphony, the orchestra was perfect. The first three movements were over, and Mr. Kraus had thought of nothing to say to improve the orchestra's performance. He kept thinking, "I've got to say something," but he could think of nothing to say. Finally, he asked the first horn to stress a certain note. When the rehearsal was over, Mr. Kraus congratulated himself in his dressing room, but then a knock sounded on his door. It was the first horn, who said, "Maestro, you know that place you asked me to accent? When we used to do it for Dr. Brahms, he always made a point of telling us to play that bit as smoothly as possible."[60]

• World-famous conductors have advantages the rest of us don't have. Arturo Toscanini was working on Beethoven's *Leonore Overture No. 2* and wasn't quite sure if the articulation of the strings was clear enough for the audience to hear. Fortunately, a world-famous composer was watching the rehearsal. Toscanini called out into the darkness of the rehearsal hall, "Rachmaninoff, can you hear?" The reply came back, "I can hear." On another occasion, Toscanini had a conversation with composer Claude Debussy in which he pointed out to the composer that many things were not clear in the composition *La Mer*. Debussy replied that it was OK for Toscanini to make changes. [61]

• Conductor Arturo Toscanini could be hard on the members of his orchestra — unless they gave him what he wanted. At a rehearsal, the Maestro was not pleased with a certain musician's performance, so he asked the musician the year he was born, the month he was born, and the day of the week he was born. On hearing the answer to his final question, Toscanini said sarcastically, "*That* was a black day for music!" The orchestra then played the piece from the beginning, and this time the musician did not offend. Toscanini beamed at the musician, and told him, "So you are not stupid. You can play well. Now I am happy. You are happy. Beethoven is happy."[62]

• Hans von Bülow once had some trouble with his kettle-drummer. At a rehearsal, he stopped and told the kettle-drummer, "*Forte*," then started the piece again. The kettle-drummer played louder, but again von Bülow stopped and told the kettle-drummer, "*Forte*," then started the piece again. The kettle-drummer again played louder, but for the third time Bülow stopped and told the kettle-drummer, "*Forte*." This time the drummer replied that he couldn't play any louder. Bülow replied, "I didn't ask you to play louder. You play *fortissimo* — the score only calls for *forte*."[63]

• In the early days of radio, during a live radio broadcast, the lights in the studio went out, and the NBC Musical Director, Frank Black, had to quickly think what to do. He immediately announced that the orchestra would play "The Stars and Stripes Forever," knowing that this was a piece of music that any orchestra should be able to play without looking at printed music. To fill the time left in the broadcast, the orchestra played the music over and over and over. At the end of the scheduled broadcast, the announcer told the radio audience, "Frank Black and the orchestra have played "The Stars and Stripes ... *Forever*." [64]

• Although the horn is a brass instrument, it cannot sound as strong as the trombone. When Fritz Reiner was rehearsing the Philadelphia Orchestra, he kept demanding more and more volume from the horns. Finally, first horn Anton Horner went over to Maestro Reiner, grabbed his thumb, squeezed it until it turned purple, and then said, "This is what is happening to us — circulation is cut off, and lips become numb."[65]

• Spanish cellist Pablo Casals was one of the world's greatest musicians. When he was a young, unknown musician, he performed privately for Charles Lamoureux, an important French conductor. Mr. Casals played the Lalo concerto from memory, and when he had finished playing, Mr. Lamoureux had tears in his eyes. He told Mr. Casals, "My dear boy, you are one of the elect."[66]

• Conductor Frederic Prausnitz enjoyed joking with his orchestra. After a dance rehearsal at which Mr. Prausnitz' orchestra played, choreographer José Limón told him that he was pleased with how the musicians had played. Mr. Prausnitz called out, "Orchestra! Mr. Limón just paid you a compliment and you didn't even hear him. He said you are doing very well. I say you talk too much!"[67]

Critics

• Sometimes a person is acclaimed as "the greatest" because there is little basis for comparison. For example, violinist Jan Kubelik was acclaimed as "the greatest" during his first tour of the United States, but when impresario Sol Hurok brought him back to the United States in 1923, several people thought that he had slipped a little. However, Sol Elman, the father of violinist Mischa Elman, thought differently. He said, "My dear friends, Kubelik played the Paganini concerto tonight as splendidly as ever he did. Today you have a different standard. You have Elman, Heifetz, and the rest. All of you have developed and grown in artistry, technique, and, above all, in knowledge and appreciation. The point is: you know more; not that Kubelik plays less well."[68]

• In Batignano, Italy, Musica nel Chiostro (Music in the Cloisters) produced *The Turn of the Screw*. Singers in the opera often stopped by the kitchen to help with preparations of the meal, where they often sang as they worked. One day, with the right number and right kinds of voices present, they sang Act II of *The Marriage of Figaro*. As they sang, Adam Pollack was in a nearby room speaking with the most influential opera critic in Rome, attempting to get him to come to *The Turn of the Screw*. The critic heard the singing in the background and asked, "Is that rehearsals going on?" "No," Mr. Pollack replied, "that's just the kitchen staff." The critic came, and he gave *The Turn of the Screw* a glowing review.[69]

• The first time Frances Alda sang at the Metropolitan Opera, she received very bad reviews. Afterward, her throat was sore, so she sought the advice of a physician. Dr. Clarence Rice examined her throat, and then told her, "Here is my prescription. Forget about your throat. Go down to the Library in Astor Place, ask for the newspaper files, and read the reviews of Emma Eames', of Farrar's, of Jean de Reszké's first performance. If your throat still bothers you tomorrow, come back and let me look at it." She followed the physician's advice and discovered that the same critics who had hated her, had also hated these other great opera singers. Her throat problem disappeared.[70]

• When Mary Garden became director of the Chicago Grand Opera Company, she immediately began to receive anonymous threats, and sometimes people sent her knives or guns in the mail. Once, she even received a box of bullets, along with this note: "Remember that there should be twelve bullets in this box. Count them. There are only eleven. The twelfth is for you." She laughed at such threats.[71]

• After the opening of the musical *Girl Crazy*, in which Ethel Merman got her big break, she met George Gershwin for lunch. Ms. Merman hadn't read the reviews yet, but Mr. Gershwin showed them to her — the critics raved about her performance and said that a star had been born. Ms. Merman, who never lacked self-confidence, said, "It figured."[72]

• While singing at the Metropolitan Opera, soprano Renata Tebaldi was surprised when the critics left before the end of the opera to write their reviews and meet their deadline. She asked, "Do they never stay to the end of the opera? How can they tell what has happened?"[73]

• George Bernard Shaw could be quite caustic in his criticism. One day, he attended a recital by an Italian quartet. During a pause in the recital, a friend remarked, "These men have been playing together for 12 years." Mr. Shaw replied, "Surely we have been here longer than that."[74]

• Blues singer Muddy Waters first heard his voice on a recording in the early 1940s. His impression of his voice was positive; afterward, he said, "I thought, man, this boy can sing the blues. And I was surprised because I didn't know I sang like that."[75]

Dance

• Sir Thomas Beecham conducted the score by Frederick Delius for *Romeo and Juliet* very slowly — much more slowly than other conductors. During performances of *Romeo and Juliet* by Ballet Theatre, two men at the close of a number held ballerina Alicia Markova in the air. After a short pause, the music was supposed to start again and the two men would lower Ms. Markova to the ground. However, during one performance, Sir Thomas held the pause a very long time. Because the men were getting tired holding her — their arms were trembling — Ms. Markova whispered that they should lower her to the ground before the music started again. After the performance, Sir Thomas explained why he had paused so long: He had thought that the pose of the two men holding Ms. Markova in the air was very pretty, and so he had paused a long time to let the audience enjoy it.[76]

• While young ballerina Darci Kistler was taking classes at the School of American Ballet, Lyn Stanford was the pianist for the classes taught by Stanley Williams. At the end of class, when all the ballerinas were tired, Mr. Stanford played popular songs such as "A Spoonful of Sugar Makes the Medicine Go Down" — with a ballet beat.[77]

Death

• Rabbi Shlomo Carlebach, aka the father of modern Jewish music, once saved the life of a would-be suicide while on a musical tour in Copenhagen. He saw an emotionally distraught young woman who was being taunted by some teenagers on a beach suddenly walk into the water and swim out to sea. He swam out after her, calling to her and begging her to return to shore. Finally, he shouted out to her, "What about me? You're not only going to kill yourself, but you're going to kill me as well. Please, if you go any further, I'll never make it back. I won't have the strength to swim back." The young woman heard him, turned around, and they swam back to shore together.[78]

• Sir Thomas Beecham, the famed conductor, once desperately needed a set designer and asked David Webster, "How is Aubrey Hammond these days?" Mr. Webster, who knew that Mr. Hammond was now the *late* Mr. Hammond, said, "He is as well as can be expected." When Sir Thomas ordered, "Well, ring him up," Mr. Webster replied, "Sir Thomas, I don't think he would like to be disturbed."[79]

• When Leonard Bernstein died, Rudolf Nureyev was seen leaving the funeral service. A reporter asked him, "What do you think of Leonard Bernstein's death, Mr. Baryshnikov?" Mr. Nureyev was saddened by Mr. Bernstein's death but later he got a kick out of the reporter's mistake, saying, "Wrong again. They got it wrong again."[80]

• Even after releasing the single "It's Like That" in March of 1983, the members of the rap group Run-D.M.C. weren't sure that their music career would continue, so they enrolled in college. Jay "Jam Master Jay" Mizell later explained, "Everyone said rap was a fad. I knew death wasn't a fad, so I majored in mortuary science."[81]

• Ludwig van Beethoven died during a tremendous thunderstorm. A lightning bolt flashed across Vienna at 5:45 p.m. on March 26, 1827, and thunder rocked the air. Lying on his deathbed, Beethoven opened his eyes, clenched his fist, shook it at the heavens, and died.[82]

Education

• At age 13, William F. Buckley was sent to an English boarding school, where his piano teacher offered to teach him the first movement of Beethoven's "Moonlight Sonata." However, William's old piano teacher had warned him that playing the "Moonlight Sonata" before one was ready was simply wrong; therefore, he wrote her for permission to learn to play its first movement. Quickly, he received a letter from her in reply, and she did not give him permission to learn the first movement. She explained that if one was unable to learn the difficult third movement, then one should not learn the first movement. She also explained that the first movement required a "maturity" that William was too young to have acquired. Mr. Buckley writes that this letter helped teach him that "good music is a very serious business."[83]

• Trey Reely, the band director of Paragould High School in Paragould, Arkansas, follows a tradition of punishing students by telling them to get a pinecone when they do something wrong. Pine trees line the band practice field, and the naughty student runs to the side of the field, picks up a pinecone, and then brings it back. Once, Mr. Reely told the band that he would not keep them late one practice, but he did keep them late; therefore, after practice his students made him get a pinecone.[84]

• A mother once asked George Bernard Shaw what musical instrument her son should learn to play, adding that she hoped that Shaw could specify an instrument which would save her the discomfort of the early learning stage during which her son would not have mastered the instrument. Shaw suggested that her son learn to play the bagpipes, saying they sound exactly the same whether or not the musician knows how to play them.[85]

• As a student, comic singer Anna Russell was so bored with her history lessons that she transformed her notes into jingles, set them to music, and began singing them. When other students found out what she was doing, they also asked for copies of her jingles, and soon the jingles were being sung all over the school. That year's graduating class was noisy, but it achieved the school's all-time high scores in history. [86]

• Woody Allen largely taught himself how to play jazz trumpet by listening to and imitating the records of jazz great George Lewis. After Mr. Allen recorded the soundtrack for his movie *Sleeper* with the Preservation Hall Jazz Band and the New Orleans Funeral and Ragtime Orchestra, trombonist Jim Robinson said to him, "Did anyone ever tell you that you sound like my friend George Lewis?"[87]

• When she was young, Mariah Carey had an unsupportive teacher. Mariah told her teacher that she wanted to be a singer when she grew up, and the teacher snapped, "There are millions of people out there who can sing. What makes you any different? Don't get your hopes up." Fortunately, her mother told her to follow her dreams, and Ms. Carey recorded five Number One hits in a row.[88]

• As a young music student, Geraldine Farrar wrote Lilli Lehmann several times, asking to become one of her students, but she never received a reply from the great vocalist. Finally, Geraldine's mother wrote Ms. Lehmann, and she received an immediate reply. Ms. Lehmann had received all of Geraldine's letters, but the handwriting had been so bad that she was unable to read them.[89]

• Ermanno Wolf-Ferrari was a brilliant student at the Munich Conservatory. An exam asked the students to compose a fugue in four voices. Instead, Mr. Wolf-Ferrari composed a double-fugue in eight voices, for which he used an original first subject. As a second subject, he used the theme his teacher had given on the test.[90]

• British actor Stanley Holloway once mentioned to Jascha Heifetz that he was looking for a school for his son, and he named one school that accepted pupils very early in their life — at two and a half years old. "Two and a half," Mr. Heifetz said. "What's he going to do till then? Just loaf around?"[91]

• Charlie "Bird" Parker is one of the greatest jazz saxophone players of all time, but even he had to learn how to play well. When he was a teenager, he played some jam sessions with local musicians. At one jam session, he made numerous mistakes and the drummer threw his cymbals at him in disgust.[92]

• As a child, rocker Bruce Springsteen hated school. While attending St. Rose of Lima Grade School, he was totally out of control. Finally, his teacher found a way to control him. She made him sit in a trashcan which she kept under her desk.[93]

• Giacomo Puccini was taught music by his Uncle Fortunato, who used to kick him in the leg if he sang a note incorrectly. Due to this training, when the adult Puccini heard a wrong note, his leg would involuntarily jerk.[94]

Fans

• Even celebrities can make fools of themselves when meeting other celebrities. Gay author Michael Thomas Ford grew up admiring Lisa and Wendy, two women musicians in pop star Prince's band, and he watched for them each time a Prince video was shown on MTV and attended Prince concerts just so he could see them. When he discovered that a friend of his knew them, he asked that a dinner be held so he could meet them. At the dinner, the first thing he said to his idols after being introduced was, "I love you" — something he had wanted to tell them for a decade. Wendy laughed, and Lisa held his hand and replied, "We love you, too." The evening was fun, and Wendy and Lisa were fabulous, even without the teased hair and makeup they wore in the MTV videos and during concerts.[95]

• In 1982, Rabbi Shlomo Carlebach, aka the Singing Rabbi, was in Jerusalem, where he was seen by some boys from the international Jewish boys camp known as Camp Sdei Chemed. Because Rabbi Shlomo was a Jewish celebrity, their mouths fell open and they stared at him. Rabbi Shlomo noticed the boys and crossed the street to greet them. The boys asked their counselor to request that Rabbi Shlomo sing a few songs for them, but he pointed out that it was nearly midnight and that the good Rabbi was probably going home tired after giving a concert. However, since the boys were insistent, he requested the songs. Rabbi Shlomo replied, "Sure! With pleasure! — and he gave them a two-hour concert under the stars.[96]

• Enrico Caruso was so popular that audiences kept applauding him long after he wished to leave the opera house, thus forcing him to come up with hints for the members of the audience to go home. He sometimes appeared at the final curtain carrying his wig in his hand — or dressed in an overcoat, with his hat and his walking stick in one arm and a lit cigar in the other hand. He was so famous that whenever he went for a walk, he was forced to have a car follow him so that he could be driven away if mobs of admirers tried to surround him.[97]

• Tom Jones, the male sex symbol and singing star, once was on tour in Mobile, Alabama. A limousine with a woman driver picked him up and drove away. They drove and drove, but the nightclub where he was to perform was still not in sight. Finally, Mr. Jones asked the driver, "Where are you taking me?" She replied, "I'm taking you to my house." She wasn't kidding. When they arrived at the driver's house, 25 of her women friends were waiting to meet Mr. Jones.[98]

• Susannah Cibber sang at the first performance of George Frideric Handel's *Messiah* on April 23, 1742, in Dublin. Her emotion as she sang was overwhelming, and after she finished singing "He was Despised," the chancellor of St. Patrick's Cathedral, Dr. Patrick Delany, shouted, "Woman, for this, be all thy sins forgiven." (According to music historians, Ms. Cibber had quite a few sins to be forgiven for.) [99]

• Herman's Hermits was a very popular pop group in the 1960s, recording such hits as "Mrs. Brown, You've Got a Lovely Daughter," "Dandy," and "I'm Henry VIII, I Am." In 2000, they performed before nostalgic audiences often consisting of women in their 40s and 50s. According to lead singer Peter Noone, "Girls used to throw underwear at us. We still get some, but it's bigger than it used to be."[100]

• There was so much screaming at the early Beatles concerts in the U.S. that the Beatles couldn't hear themselves play. Once, the Beatles were discussing their performance after a concert. When the name of a certain song came up, Ringo said, "We didn't play that song tonight." The other Beatles looked at each other, and then said, "*We* did."[101]

• After singing the part of Sieglinde in Wagner's *Die Walküre*, American soprano Olive Fremstad was cornered by a fan who told her, "I used to be so confused by Wagner, but tonight I really believe I understand it all!" Ms. Fremstad replied, "You are more fortunate than I, who have given my whole life to the study and still know so little." [102]

• At a party given by George Gershwin, the composer spent a lot of time talking about himself. During a pause in the Gershwin monologue, Oscar Levant asked, "Tell me, George, if you had to do it all over, would you fall in love with yourself again?"[103]

Chapter 3: From Fathers to Language

Fathers

• Songwriter Sammy Cahn ("Love and Marriage," "Three Coins in the Fountain," "Call Me Irresponsible," and "I'll Walk Alone") remembers attending Yom Kippur services with his father. Like the other Jews, his father was beating his breast and saying the *Al Chet*, a long list of sins that is recited on Yom Kippur. Suddenly, his father, who was not known to be a funny man, turned to him and whispered, "I don't know why I'm beating my breast. I haven't done anything."[104]

• Early in her career, Melissa Etheridge was given a lot of support by her father. She picked up early experience singing in bar bands, and her father would sit all night at whatever bar she was performing in because young Melissa was underage.[105]

Flowers

• Adelina Patti insisted on being admired. She once sang with the bass singer Luigi Lablache, who scored a huge success and was given much applause and many wreaths. Angry that her own effort was not more admired, Ms. Patti seized one of Mr. Lablache's wreaths, and then told the astonished audience, "I have well deserved it myself!"[106]

• Before performances, jazz singer Billie Holiday often used a curling iron on her hair. Unfortunately, she made a mistake one day and burned some of it, so she wore a big white gardenia to cover the burned place. She liked the look so much that she continued to wear white gardenias in her hair long after it had grown back.[107]

Food

• Author Peg Bracken knows a woman who prepared a luncheon for the conductor of her city's symphony orchestra. The luncheon was truly marvelous, and in the middle of the table were two large silver containers: one filled with fruit salad, and the other filled with a curry mayonnaise. The hostess lifted the lid of the container filled with the curry mayonnaise, and a mouse jumped out onto the conductor's plate. Ms. Bracken says, "My friend is all right. When I saw her last week, she was sitting up, and we think she'll be taking a little nourishment any day now."[108]

• During a feud between Maria Callas and Renata Tebaldi, many opera fans took sides, and they became known as Tebaldiani and Callasiani, according to whom they supported. At least one fan took the feud much too seriously. In the summer of 1959, a woman friend of writer Victor Seroff dined at a restaurant near La Scala, and she discovered a nail in her spaghetti. She showed the nail to her waiter, who explained, "They must have taken you for Madame Callas."[109]

• Things do not always go well at musical performances, even when they are conducted by Arturo Toscanini. After a poor performance at La Scala, he returned home in a foul mood. As usual, a late supper had been prepared for the Toscanini family, but Maestro Toscanini barred the way to the dining room, saying, "What! You can *eat* after such a performance! Shame on you! *Shame!*" That night, everybody in the Toscanini household went to bed hungry.[110]

• Ludwig van Beethoven once walked into the Swan, his favorite restaurant, sat at a table, and began to jot down some musical ideas in a notebook he carried. Because he was so busy writing, the waiters left him in peace, knowing that he wanted it that way. After a long time had passed, Beethoven looked up from his notebook, and then asked a waiter to bring him his bill. The waiter was forced to explain to Beethoven that he hadn't ordered yet.[111]

• Blues singer Bessie Smith fell in love with police officer Jackie Gee, and after he was shot in the line of duty, she was determined to take care of him. After he was discharged from the hospital, she cooked pork chops, black-eyed peas, cornmeal, collard greens, and everything that goes with them. Mr. Gee ate more than his fill, and the next day he was back in the hospital — he had eaten so much that his stitches had burst.[112]

• Ballet is an enchanting art; however, sometimes the audience is unaware of what occurs on stage. While touring with the Ballet Russe de Monte Carlo, the dancers would occasionally whisper among themselves during the last act of *The Nutcracker* or other ballet. While the audience listened to the music and watched the dancing in wonderment, the dancers would be discussing where to eat after the curtain fell.[113]

• Early in his career, Louis Armstrong worked as a jazz musician on a riverboat. He watched as a fellow musician almost starved himself to get money to invest in cotton. The man went hungry, saved his money, invested it in a cotton crop — and lost all his money when the crop failed because of boll weevils. Mr. Armstrong decided then and there that he would never be rich — but he would be fat.[114]

Friends

• Who drummer Keith Moon and Monty Python member Graham Chapman were great friends and great drinkers. Mr. Chapman visited Mr. Moon one day when Mr. Moon was out of gin, Mr. Chapman's preferred alcoholic beverage. Mr. Moon ordered gin from room service, but room service was slow — so he stepped out a window, onto a 4- or 5-inch ledge, on which he made his way into a neighboring apartment, from which he burgled a bottle of gin to offer to his friend.[115]

• Opera singers hate to catch colds and the flu. While in New York, Luciano Pavarotti came down with the flu. Fellow opera singer and friend Mirella Freni felt sympathy for him, but she didn't want to catch his flu. Therefore, she made hot soup and left it outside his dressing room door. Then she ran away from the door, muttering, "*Povero amico mio, povero ragazzo*" ("My poor friend, poor boy").[116]

• Rudolf Nureyev and Leonard Bernstein lived very close to each other in the Dakota on Central Part West in New York City. In fact, their apartments were separated by a party wall, and they used to tap on the wall occasionally to say hi to each other.[117]

Gay Men

• Bette Midler began her career at a gay bathhouse, which meant that she performed in front of a lot of gay men wearing nothing but towels. This was a big opportunity for her, as the gay men treated her act with respect, although it only hinted at the superstar act Ms. Midler later created. In addition, the gay men gave Ms. Midler the freedom to experiment and be outrageous on stage. She says, "Ironically, I was freed from fear by people who, at the time, were ruled by fear." (She also says she never saw a penis in the Baths, although she admits she looked real hard.)[118]

• Popular culture has many gay icons, including Stevie Nicks of the pop group Fleetwood Mac. In New York, the Jackie 60 club holds an annual Night of a Thousand Stevies in which gay men dress as their idol. (Being a gay icon is a major compliment. It means that you live your life with flair and elegance — and you look fabulous.)[119]

Gifts

• The Beach Boys and Jan and Dean played similar kinds of surfing music. In fact, when Brian Wilson was unable to come up with a good ending for "Surf City," he gave the song to Jan Berry. Mr. Berry came up with a good ending, and then recorded it with his singing partner, Dean Torrence, and it became a No. 1 hit. Later, when the Beach Boys were recording "Barbara Ann," Mr. Torrence happened to be in the studio, and he recorded the lead vocals. However, he didn't get any credit on the album notes because according to his contract, the only group he could record for was Jan and Dean.[120]

• While performing in Paris, soprano Emma Albani received a notable gift from some young USAmerican art students. They had taken a box near the stage so that they could give her their gift: a large basket of flowers, under which they had placed an album of sketches they had created especially for her. This was quite a gift, since the young USAmerican art students — Bridgeman, Lowe, Sargent — later became famous.[121]

• In 1964, the New York Yankees, who were managed by Yogi Berra, suffered a losing season. After yet another loss, infielder Phil Linz started to play happy tunes on his harmonica on the team bus. This annoyed Yogi, so he fined Mr. Linz $200. However, when Mr. Linz signed his next Yankee contract, Yogi gave him a $200 bonus — so he could get music lessons.[122]

• While rehearsing *Norma* in San Francisco, soprano Rita Hunter ran into a problem. The props department didn't have a dagger for her character to use to murder the children in the opera, so she used a spatula with a flat rubber blade. Afterward, the stage management had the spatula inscribed and presented it to her. She treasured the gift.[123]

• British actor Stanley Holloway once appeared in the show *Crescendo* with Rex Harrison and jazz trumpeter Louis Armstrong. Mr. Armstrong gave a gift to everyone associated with the show — packets containing herbs for the bowels. According to Mr. Armstrong, the herbs were "marvelous for keeping you healthy."[124]

• In Paris, soprano Adelina Patti readily agreed to sing at a benefit for a little-known, young actress who had lost all her possessions in a fire. Later, the little-known actress made a great reputation and everyone knew the name of Sarah Bernhardt.[125]

Husbands and Wives

• Irving Berlin carried on a romance with Ellin Mackay, who was the daughter of the President of the Postal Telegraph. Unfortunately, Mr. Mackay did not appreciate Mr. Berlin's attentions to his daughter, so he approached Mr. Berlin with an offer — he would give Mr. Berlin $1 million not to interfere with Miss Mackay's future. Mr. Berlin, a very successful songwriter, made a counteroffer — he would give Mr. Mackay $2 million not to interfere with Miss Mackay's future. Eventually, Mr. Berlin and Miss Mackay were married.[126]

• After blues singer Bessie Smith married police officer Jackie Gee, she became a jealous wife. One night, she kissed him, and then performed on stage. After finishing her act, she left the stage, saw lipstick on her husband's face, and then hit him and knocked him down, demanding to know whose lipstick it was. He had to remind her that she had kissed him before she had performed and the lipstick was hers.[127]

• Tenor Mario de Candia married soprano Giulia Grisi. Theirs was a happy marriage which resulted in six daughters. One day, Ms. Grisi and her daughters were walking in a park, where they met a noble who asked her about her daughters, "These, madam, are, I suppose, your little *grisettes*." She replied, "Oh, no, sir! These are my little *marionettes*." [128]

Illegal Drugs

• Bette Midler doesn't take illegal drugs when she performs live — she's tried it with bad results. But she does make fun of people who think she takes illegal drugs when she performs live. In her 1980 world tour, she imitated an imaginary straight member of the audience saying, "Harry! Where does she get all that energy from? She must take something, Harry. What do you think she takes?" Then the Divine Miss M would say, dramatically, "I don't take anything. I'm high on life." She still remembers a voice from the real audience calling out from the balcony, "Where can I get some?"[129]

• Gangsta rap has given rap music a bad name, but of course not all rap is gangsta rap. Darryl "D.M.C." McDaniels of Run-D.M.C. is a hero of little kids in his neighborhood. They follow him around, and D.M.C. first tells them to stay in school, and then he gives them money to buy something from a deli. Many rappers are anti-drug. Grandmaster Flash wrote "White Lines" to explain how cocaine can ruin a person's life. On the record he gives his advice about getting involved with the drug: "Don't do it!"[130]

Illness

• Gustave Charpentier, French composer of the opera *Julien*, was invited to attend a performance of the opera at the Metropolitan Opera. Mr. Charpentier wanted to go, so in preparation for the sea voyage, he sailed in a boat for 15 minutes on the Seine. This short boat ride made him ill, and he declined the invitation to go to New York, having resolved to spend the rest of his life on land.[131]

• Gustav Holst wrote *At the Boar's Head* (1925) while recuperating from a head injury. He was reading Shakespeare's *Henry IV* plays and studying English folk music, when he noticed that the melody of one of the folk songs fit a passage from one of the *Henry IV* plays. Because of that happy accident, he wrote an opera using folk songs and passages from the *Henry IV* plays.[132]

Instruments

• Should junior high and high school musicians regularly clean their instruments? Trey Reely, the band director of Paragould High School in Paragould, Arkansas, thinks so. To persuade his students to do this, he tells a story that a repair technician told about a student who brought him a trombone that would not produce a sound no matter how hard he blew into it. The technician disassembled the trombone and discovered, clogging the bottom of the slide, three mice.[133]

• Mstislav Rostropovitch owns a Stradivari cello with a long scratch on a lower bout. Why hasn't he had the scratch repaired? Because the scratch was made by a very important person. Napoleon Bonaparte had asked a previous owner for permission to play the cello, and as he was sitting down, one of his spurs made the scratch.[134]

Insults

• Who drummer Keith Moon did not take criticism kindly. He once stayed at the Hyatt House on Sunset Strip in LA. Walking through the lobby, he loudly played a tape recording of a Who rehearsal. People complained to the manager, who told him, "Turn that noise off." Mr. Moon went up to his room, where he had stashed away several detonator caps that were intended to be used at a Who concert. He affixed the detonator caps to the door of his room, and then he called the manager and said he needed to talk to him immediately. The manager came to his room, knocked on his door — and Mr. Moon set off the detonator caps, exploding the door into pieces. He pointed to the pieces of the door and told the manager, "*That* was noise." Then he pointed to his tape recording of the Who rehearsal and said, "*This* is The Who."[135]

• When he was a very young man in Barcelona, cellist Pablo Casals performed in a production of *Carmen*. During intermission, a double bass player asked him what was the most beautiful part of *Carmen*. Mr. Casals mentioned both the prelude to the third act and the flower song, but the double bass player said that the most beautiful part occurred when the tenor sang, "*Vous pouvez m'arrêter. C'est moi qui qui l'ai tuée.*" Mr. Casals replied that yes, that was beautiful, but then the double bass player added, "Listen to me, Pau. That is beautiful, because when I hear that, I know that I will be going home in a few minutes." Mr. Casals said many decades later to Plácido Domingo, "Do you know, after more than eighty years, I cannot forgive that man for what he said that evening."[136]

• Adelina Patti was a very popular prima donna of the late 1880s. While on an American tour, Ms. Patti was introduced to the Governor of Missouri, General Crittenden, who was so overwhelmed at meeting her that he gave her a kiss — quite a liberty in those days. Ms. Patti later told reporters that she did not object to the kiss, seeing as how the General was "such a nice old gentleman." Ms. Patti's leading rival, Etelka Gerster, also told reporters that she saw nothing to object to in the General's kissing Ms. Patti, saying, "There is nothing wrong in a man kissing a woman old enough to be his mother."[137]

• Singer Emma Abbott was very popular around the beginning of the 20th century. Very religious, Ms. Abbott always attended church in whatever town or city she was singing. At a church in Nashville, Tennessee, the minister began to preach a sermon on the evil of show business. That made Ms. Abbott so angry that she stood up in church and denounced the minister, pointing out that many women in show business led lives as irreproachable as those of any wife in the congregation.[138]

• Violinist Fritz Kreisler was once asked by a snooty society lady to play at one of her affairs. Mr. Kreisler replied that his fee would be $3,000. The society lady agreed to the price, but told him that he must not mingle with the guests. "In that case," Mr. Kreisler said, "my fee will be $2,000."[139]

Language

• African-American diva Marian Anderson was capable of true humility. Some people regarded her use of third-person pronouns to refer to herself — "We felt we sang well" — as affected, but she disliked "I" and "me" because she felt their use implied vanity. Once, New York vocal coach Lola Hayes rode the Eighth Avenue subway on her way to a Marian Anderson concert at Town Hall; at a stop, she saw a woman who looked like Ms. Anderson board the subway. When they both got off at Town Hall, she asked, "Miss Anderson?" It was she. Today, it's difficult to imagine any music superstar taking the subway.[140]

Latin singer Mark Anthony revolutionized salsa music with his album *Todo a Su Tiempo* ("Everything in Its Time"), which merged Latin dance rhythms with 1990s pop, yet early in his music career he had trouble giving interviews to members of the Spanish-speaking media. Having been raised in New York City, Mr. Anthony was not fluent in Spanish, and therefore he had to take Spanish lessons to be prepared to give interviews in that language after his albums became huge sellers in Latin American countries.[141]

• Music can transcend cultures. Salsa music is a blend of many musical styles, including Spanish guitar, African rhythms, and North American rock, jazz, and rhythm and blues. Nevertheless, in Japan is a salsa band called Orquesta De La Luz. Its members speak Japanese, not Spanish, but sing the Spanish lyrics phonetically. People who know salsa music say that the music of Orquesta De La Luz sounds like real salsa.[142]

• Opera singer Geraldine Farrar was imperfect in French early in her career. During her first trip to France, she and her mother went to a small family hotel in Boulogne, where Geraldine — speaking stammering French — told the landlady what they needed and what they were willing to pay. The landlady — speaking perfect English — replied, "If you will only tell me in English, I can understand you better."[143]

• The music of Latino Ricky Martin is popular across the world. While on a Far East tour, he was amazed to perform in a Chinese town and hear his Chinese fans singing, "*Un, dos, tres, un pasisto pa'lante, Maria*." Mr. Martin says, "I've gotten the Chinese to speak Spanish. Who else can say that?"[144]

Chapter 4: From Mishaps to Prejudice

Mishaps

• Arturo Toscanini had a phenomenal memory as well as a phenomenal ear. Once, he decided to conduct Ernest Schelling's "Impressions from an Artist's Life," and he invited Mr. Schelling himself to play solo piano. During rehearsal, Maestro Toscanini — who never looked at a score during rehearsal, although he kept one on the stage — stopped Mr. Schelling and stated that he believed the pianist had omitted a G flat. Mr. Schelling replied, "You are right. I did omit the G flat because I never wrote a G flat at that particular point in my original score." That surprised Maestro Toscanini, so he invited Mr. Schelling to look at the score with him. After looking at the score, it was Mr. Schelling who was surprised, and he said, "Mr. Toscanini, I *did* omit the G flat. In all the times I have played this piece I *always* omitted the G flat. Since the day I wrote it, I had completely forgotten it was there."[145]

• Pianist Artur Rubinstein once objected to a movie script in which a conductor drowned out the music of a pianist during a concert. He asserted that no conductor would ever do this. Shortly afterward, he went to an appointment to make a recording with conductor Leopold Stokowski. The two men interpreted the music differently, with Mr. Rubinstein playing one way while Mr. Stokowski conducted another way — with the result that the conductor drowned out the music of the pianist. Mr. Rubinstein then told the director of the movie with the script he had objected to, "Don't bother about changing that script. I was wrong."[146]

• Lucien Muratore once sang the role of Faust with a Mephisto who was very stout. In the opera, Mephisto made a grand entrance by rising up from a trapdoor. Unfortunately, because of Mephisto's great bulk, the fit through the trapdoor was very tight and the lower part of his clothing was torn. Unaware of just what and how much he was revealing, the actor playing Mephisto sang his entrance lines: "Why do you start as you greet me? Does it frighten you to see me?" The audience was not frightened — it laughed until the curtain was drawn to enable Mephisto to cover his predicament.[147]

• Professional opera singers must be ready to deal with the unexpected on stage. On May 19, 1961, Plácido Domingo made his debut as lead singer in the role of Alfredo in Giuseppe Verdi's *La Traviata*. In the second act, a letter from Violetta was supposed to arrive for Alfredo by messenger. Looking at the door where the messenger was supposed to appear, Mr. Domingo sang, "Who's there?" No messenger appeared! Thinking quickly, Mr. Domingo sang, "No one," then he picked up a paper lying on a desk and sang, "From Violetta!" He then continued with the scene as it had been written. [148]

• Early in his career, George Kirby appeared on stage with Duke Ellington and his band. However, due to a lack of rehearsal, the band did a poor job of playing the music for Mr. Kirby's act — of course, the band was great as always when doing their own material. After their first performance together, Mr. Ellington came to Mr. Kirby and apologized for the poor performance of the piano player. Mr. Kirby said, "But you're the piano player." "I know," Mr. Ellington said. "That's what I meant — the piano player screwed up!" Mr. Kirby and Duke Ellington's band then practiced together, and the next performance was perfect.[149]

• Opera/lieder singer Kathleen Ferrier occasionally made mental lapses, forgetting a phrase as she sang. She once forgot some of the words to Handel's "Where'er You Walk." So instead of singing, "All things flourish, where'er you turn your eyes," she sang the only thing she could think of, which was, "All things flourish, where'er they eat the grass." This normally wouldn't be too bad, but the phrase which she couldn't remember appeared three times in the song, and by the time she had finished singing it, her face was bright red.[150]

• Coloratura soprano Lily Pons was a perfectionist. Before singing in an auditorium, she noticed that red velvet curtains hung at the back of the stage. Concerned that the curtains would absorb too much of the sound of her voice, she insisted that they be taken down. They were taken down, but unfortunately this revealed a large sign that was clearly visible as Ms. Pons sang during her concert: "RESTROOMS — THIS WAY."[151]

• Meredith Willson (the writer of *The Music Man*) and his wife were just leaving the Brown Derby in Hollywood when they ran into a producer whom they knew. The producer greeted Mr. Willson enthusiastically and complimented him on his fine head of hair. Reciprocating, Mr. Willson complimented the producer on his hair and grabbed a handful of it — only to pull off the producer's toupee. [152]

• Tenor Franco Corelli takes music seriously. At home, Mr. Corelli became so frustrated while trying unsuccessfully to play a certain phrase that he jumped up from the piano then smashed his fist through a closet door. He and his wife were unsuccessful at freeing his arm, so they were forced to call a carpenter for help.[153]

• During a performance of *High Spirits*, the musical version of his *Blithe Spirit*, Noël Coward was bothered by an usher who kept switching on and off a flashlight in an attempt to get another usher's attention. "Good God," he moaned, "will somebody please go up there and kill Tinker Bell!" (In performances of *Peter Pan*, Tinker Bell is portrayed by a light.)[154]

• Years ago, guests on *The Mike Douglas Show* included pianist Roger Williams and the fashion director of *Playboy*, Robert L. Green. Mr. Green told Mr. Williams, "Although I have never met you, I've heard you tinkling many times." Mr. Williams replied, "I've been tinkling since I was a little child."[155]

• Oscar Levant was performing on stage in a concert when a telephone began ringing — and ringing — off stage. When he came to a quiet place in the piano piece he was playing, he told the audience, "If that's for me, tell them I'm busy."[156]

Money

• Colonel James H. Mapleson was the impresario of a traveling opera company starring Adelina Patti, who refused to perform for less than $5,000 — always paid in advance. One day, Colonel Mapleson was short of money, so he gave her agent $4,000, and said that he hoped she would perform. Ms. Patti's agent spoke with her, and then reported she had said that for $4,000, she would consent to put on her costume, but she would leave her shoes off — and in the meantime he should get more money. Later, Colonel Mapleson arrived with another $800, and Ms. Patti put on one shoe. Finally, Colonel Mapleson came up with another $200, and Ms. Patti put on her other shoe, and then gave a fabulous performance.[157]

• In the 15th century, Josquin des Prez was an Italian composer of motets — religious songs sung without accompaniment. When the Duke of Ferrara was very slow in giving Josquin a raise he had been promised, Josquin wrote a motet on the religious text, "Remember thy word unto thy servant." The Duke got the message, came up with the promised raise, and Josquin then wrote a motet on the religious text, "Lord, thou hast dealt graciously with thy servant."[158]

• Joe Frisco was a comic who, down on his luck, ran across his old friend Bing Crosby at the horse races and borrowed $100. Fortunately, his luck changed. He bet the $100 on a long shot, won, and treated his friends to dinner at a restaurant. When Bing walked into the restaurant, Mr. Frisco pulled out a $100 bill, handed it to Bing, and said, "Here, kid, sing something."[159]

• Early in his career as an opera singer, Luciano Pavarotti didn't make much money. However, he got a job with an opera company in Holland that paid him all the money it owed him at the end of the several weeks he sang there. Mr. Pavarotti took his pay home and used it to cover the bedroom — even sticking money to the walls — as a surprise for his wife.[160]

• Oboe player Bruno Labate was not afraid of conductors and occasionally spoke harshly to them. When another member of the orchestra asked about his lack of fear, Mr. Labate answered, "I should be afraid? I with $75,000 in the bank?"[161]

• For many years, Roy Henderson was the voice teacher of opera/lieder singer Kathleen Ferrier. Following a concert at which they both sang, Ms. Ferrier's check was mistakenly handed to him. He looked at it and discovered that the pupil was being paid more than the teacher.[162]

• A friend of Russell Sherman's piano teacher told him that someone driving a garbage truck probably made more money than he did playing the piano. The piano teacher replied, "Perhaps, but somehow I'd rather play the piano."[163]

Mothers

• Harpo Marx got his nickname (before Hitler's rise to power, Harpo's real name was Adolf; after Hitler's rise to power, Harpo changed his name to Arthur) because he played the harp. Apparently, lots of nursing mothers felt that harp music would be soothing to their infants, so they seated themselves by Harpo whenever he performed live. Harpo used to play soothing music for a while, and then suddenly hit a sharp chord just so he could watch the mothers jump, pulling their nipples out of their infants' mouths.[164]

• Jazz great Duke Ellington loved his mother and bought her expensive gifts — a fur coat, strings of pearls, a fancy limousine complete with chauffeur. Whenever she protested his extravagance, he would tell her, "If you don't take these things, I won't work."[165]

Names

• The premiere of *Madama Butterfly* at La Scala was a disaster — the opening-night audience hated the opera, which is now regarded as a classic. Following the premiere Giacomo Puccini even took back the score so that the opera couldn't be played there a second night. However, at least a few people loved the opera. Later, Puccini heard of a Lucca shopkeeper who had named his daughter "Butterfly" even though the clerk who had registered the infant's name asked, "Do you want to brand your child with the name of a failure?" Puccini was so touched by the tribute that he asked the father to visit him, and so the father did — he also brought along his baby daughter and 50 or 60 of their relatives.[166]

• The baritone Lawrence Tibbett once stopped at a record shop to buy a recording of his Prologue to *Pagliacci*. He asked for the record, but the sales clerk said, "There is no such recording." Mr. Tibbett explained that he knew the record to exist, as he had made it, but the clerk insisted, "We have no such name on our list." Mr. Tibbett then spelled his name, and at last the clerk knew it. She explained, "We call that Teebay. Do you really pronounce it Tibbett?" "Why not?" Mr. Tibbett replied. "I am an American, not a Frenchman."[167]

• Josef Haydn was once asked by a Viennese butcher to compose a minuet that could be played at the butcher's daughter's wedding. A kind man, Haydn agreed, and he presented the butcher with a minuet the following day. Later, Haydn heard his minuet being played in the street outside his window. Looking out, he saw the butcher with an ox — the butcher liked the minuet so much that he had decided to present Haydn with the ox. Haydn's minuet became known as the "Minuet of the Ox."[168]

• Jazz genius Miles Davis paid little attention to audiences, preferring instead to turn his back on them and play while facing his musicians. For this reason, and because of his brooding personality, people sometimes called him "The Prince of Darkness."[169]

• When Nat Cole was a young entertainer, he needed work. To get one job, he was forced to wear a gold paper crown and call himself "King" Cole. As soon as he could, he got rid of the crown, but forever after, he was known as Nat King Cole.[170]

Parties

• For New Year's Day of 1919, Enrico Caruso and his wife, Dorothy, invited 1,000 people to an afternoon reception at their home, but 3,000 people showed up. Neither host said anything, as Enrico thought the 2,000 extra people were Dorothy's friends, and Dorothy thought the 2,000 extra people were Enrico's friends. Neither host was able to eat because they were too busy greeting people, until finally they stole away to their private rooms to eat sandwiches. Although the invitations said the reception would last from 4 to 7 p.m., the last guests finished dancing at 3 a.m.[171]

• After a Led Zeppelin party in which 30 televisions were thrown out of hotel windows, the band's lawyer, Danny Goldberg, counted out $9,000 in cash and handed it to the hotel manager, who said, "No hard feelings. I'd kind of like to throw a TV out of the window, myself." Mr. Goldberg counted out another $300, handed it to the hotel manager, and said, "Be our guest."[172]

People with Handicaps

• Despite losing his right arm in World War I, Paul Wittgenstein continued playing the piano. He played the melody of the right hand using his forefinger and left thumb, and to play a chord he broke it up into two notes, but by making clever use of the piano pedal he was still able to give the impression of playing the whole chord. Of course, little music was written for the left hand only. However, several composers, including Benjamin Britten, Paul Hindemith, Sergei Prokofieff, Maurice Ravel, and Richard Strauss, wrote music for the left hand only so Mr. Wittgenstein could play it. Far from being a mere curiosity, Mr. Wittgenstein played concerts for more than 40 years, wrote a three-volume book titled *School for the Left Hand* of pieces arranged for the left hand, and recorded two albums: *Paul Wittgenstein plays Piano Music for the Left Hand* and *Transcriptions for Piano Left Hand*.[173]

• Belly dancer Mésmera once performed for musician Stevie Wonder. She made music for him by clicking her tiny zill cymbals, which he enjoyed, but because Mr. Wonder is blind, he was missing the dance. Therefore, she put his hands on her hips so he could feel the movements of the dance. Of course, she didn't put his hands anywhere else, and because Mr. Wonder is a gentleman, he didn't try to put his hands anywhere else.[174]

• George Shearing is one of the few people who can ethically get away with playing with marked cards. This famous pianist is blind, and he uses cards marked in Braille.[175]

Pianists

• Russian pianist Vladimir de Pachmann sometimes enjoyed fussing with his piano seat. He would come out in front of an audience, pretend that his seat wasn't the right height, raise it, lower it, try placing books of various sizes on the seat — then he would put a single sheet of music on the seat, sit, and start playing. Occasionally, he would play a difficult piece by Chopin — the *Sonata in B Flat Minor* — then tell the audience, "I play that better than anybody in the world."[176]

• Before giving a concert, Sviatoslav Richter was invited to try the piano. Mr. Richter sat briefly at the piano, and then rose and said that he was satisfied. When asked why he didn't actually play the piano, he replied that he would not because he was always disappointed by the sound.[177]

• At a dance rehearsal, the pianist was having trouble finding the correct chord for a difficult section of the Schoenberg Second Symphony. Choreographer José Limón came over, placed his fingers on the correct keys, smiled, and said, "This is the chord, my friend."[178]

• Oscar Levant was set to play the Brahms Concerto for the movie *Humoresque*, but the producer, Jerry Wald, asked him if he could cut the concerto from eight minutes to two. Mr. Levant replied, "Sure, I can do it — but you'll be hearing from Brahms in the morning."[179]

Police

• While in Amsterdam, famous violinist Fritz Kreisler saw a music shop displaying several violins in the window. On a lark, he decided to see how much the proprietor would offer him for his own very valuable violin: a Guarneri. The proprietor looked over the violin, excused himself, left for a moment, and returned with a police officer, whom he told, "Arrest this man. He has stolen Fritz Kreisler's violin." Mr. Kreisler had left his identification papers at his hotel, so to prove his identity, he played the violin. The music shop proprietor listened, and then said, "Nobody but Kreisler could play that beautifully."[180]

• Texas Guinan was the hostess of the El Fay Club on West Forty-fifth Street in New York City. This club was frequently raided, and whenever federal agents came in to make yet more arrests, the club's band would start playing "The Prisoner's Song."[181]

Practical Jokes

• Eastman Boomer, the agent of comic singer Anna Russell, was a practical joker. He frequently told Ms. Russell that a notable personality such as Arturo Toscanini was staying at her hotel and wanted to meet her — but this always turned out not to be true. One day, Boomer called her and said the great conductor Leopold Stokowski was coming over to meet her. Of course, Ms. Russell didn't believe him, so she put her hair up in curlers and put cold cream on her face. When a knock sounded on the door, she opened it, expecting to see Boomer — but standing before her was Maestro Stokowski.[182]

• Leo Slezak knew an operatic tenor who continually boasted of his prowess in billiards, so Mr. Slezak decided to play a joke on him. He knew a professional billiards player by the name of Pfeiler and arranged to have Mr. Pfeiler play billiards with the tenor, who had never heard of Mr. Pfeiler. In the game, Mr. Pfeiler allowed the tenor to get ahead, and then he dazzled the tenor with brilliance. As he was shooting ball after ball into the pockets, a waiter entered the room and told the tenor that Mr. Pfeiler had said for him to hold the tenor's cue stick until the game was over.[183]

• In Richard Wagner's *Siegfried* is a scene in which Siegfried approaches the sleeping Brünnhilde, removes her breastplate, and sees the words "*Das ist kein Mann.*" Tenor Alberto Remedios tells a story about a production in which Siegfried approached a mischievous sleeping Brünnhilde. When Siegfried removed her breastplate, he saw the words, "Do not disturb."[184]

Prejudice

• As a teenager, African-American diva Grace Bumbry won a voice contest sponsored by a local radio station, KMOX. The prizes included a $1,000 bond and a scholarship to the St. Louis Institute of Music. Unfortunately, the people who ran the St. Louis Institute of Music were unhappy when they learned that Ms. Bumbry was black, so they offered her only a few private voice lessons and would not let her join the student body. Ms. Bumbry's mother, Melzia, was outraged, and refused to allow her daughter to be treated so badly. The story does have a happy ending. KMOX executive Roland Hyland was embarrassed by what had happened and helped Ms. Bumbry get on Arthur Godfrey's *Talent Scouts*, where Mr. Godfrey predicted a brilliant future for her. After her appearance on the TV show, scholarship offers poured in, and Ms. Bumbry ended up attending Boston University, and then Northwestern University. Later, she made a name for herself as a famous opera singer.[185]

• African-American singer Marian Anderson used to perform while being accompanied by a white musician, Kosti Vehanen, on piano. Once, a racist white woman asked Mr. Vehanen if he was ashamed to be traveling with an African-American singer. Mr. Vehanen replied that Ms. Anderson was welcome at some places where she, the white woman, would not be welcome. Indignant, the white woman asked him to name one such place. Mr. Vehanen replied that Ms. Anderson had recently been invited to the White House, where she would sing, but that if the white woman were to try to enter the White House for the performance, she would be refused admittance.[186]

• In 1948 — back in the Jim Crow days — Gene Norman hired an assistant to promote a concert by the great African-American jazz singer Billie Holiday. The assistant received a telephone call by the entertainment editor of a newspaper, who asked, "What color is Billie Holiday? I can't tell for sure from this mat you sent me, and you know, we don't run pictures of colored people." The assistant was stunned, and she let Mr. Norman handle the call. Mr. Norman told the entertainment editor, "The last time I saw Miss Holiday, sir, she was a lovely shade of soft purple with the most exquisite orange polka dots I've ever seen," then he hung up the telephone.[187]

• When African-American gospel singer Mahalia Jackson decided to move into a white suburb, she discovered that no one wanted to sell their home to her, so she asked a real estate agent for help. The real estate agent advertised that the Queen of Gospel wanted to buy a home, and a white dentist stepped forward and said, "I'll be proud to sell my home to Mahalia." She bought the home and moved in, but her white neighbors were unhappy and harassed her, although a Catholic priest went door to door, imploring them to show tolerance. Soon, the whites moved out, and the suburb became an upper middle-class African-American neighborhood.[188]

• Singer Nat King Cole was black, and some white people didn't like it when he moved into their neighborhood. They held a meeting with him and explained that they didn't want "undesirables" in the neighborhood. Mr. Cole replied, "Neither do I, and if I see anybody undesirable coming in here, I'll be the first to complain." Some of the white people complained to the real estate agent who had sold Mr. Cole the house and asked, "Don't you check out the people you sell to?" She replied, "I sure do. As soon as they walk in the door, I ask them, 'Have you got the down payment?'"[189]

• During his career, African-American actor/singer Paul Robeson spoke out for equality and justice. Because of Mr. Robeson's outspokenness, the United States government persecuted him by making him testify before the House UnAmerican Activities Committee and by revoking his passport. Near the end of Mr.

Robeson's life, another African-American actor/singer, Harry Belafonte, asked him if the fight for freedom had been worth the cost. Mr. Robeson replied, "Make no mistake — there is no aspect of what I have done that wasn't worth it."[190]

• Billie Holiday's song "Strange Fruit" was an anti-lynching song — the "strange fruit" of the title was a reference to corpses of lynched African-Americans hanging from trees. Some people, including her mother, worried that the song would stir up trouble for her, but Billie said, "Listen, I'm proud to be singing an anti-lynching song. Someday there'll be a better world for our people." Her mother said, "Perhaps, but you won't be alive to see it." Billie replied, "Maybe not, but when it happens I'm going to be dancing in my grave."[191]

• At one time in England, professional musicians attended musical parties at which they performed but at which a cord was strung across the room. The purpose of the cord, of course, was to separate the musicians from the guests. At one party, operatic bass Luigi Lablache was speaking with someone on the other side of the cord when suddenly and quietly he untied the cord and let it drop to the floor. Thereafter, no more cords were used at musical parties in London.[192]

• During the Jim Crow days of legalized segregation, jazz singer Billie Holiday frequently had difficulty finding lodging while touring in the South. During a tour with the Artie Shaw Orchestra — Mr. Shaw and many of his musicians were white — Ms. Holiday got into one segregated hotel after having a red dot painted on her forehead. The hotel management thought she was from India and allowed her to stay. [193]

• Eartha Kitt once made a reservation at a London hotel, but when she walked into the hotel, and the clerk saw that she was black, he refused her a room. Ms. Kitt knew the reason she was refused a room, so she told the clerk that she wasn't black — she was Spanish. The clerk wasn't convinced. Sneering, he said, "So say something in Spanish." Ms. Kitt replied, "*Adios*, motherf—," and walked out.[194]

• Early in her career, when Lena Horne was singing with Charlie Barnet's band, she ran into a problem getting housing because of Jim Crow. When everyone checked into a hotel, Mr. Barnet told the clerks that Ms. Horne was a Cuban singer, while the members of the band helped with the deception by speaking nonsense that sounded like Spanish.[195]

• In 1950, André Previn played jazz in Baltimore with a couple of African-American musicians. Afterward, he went into a diner, where a couple of white men asked him, "Why the hell don't you play with your own kind?" Mr. Previn replied, "Well, to tell you the truth, I wanted to, but I couldn't find two other Jews that swing."[196]

• The noted heterosexual (and inter-species dater) Kermit the Frog and lesbian singer k.d. lang once guested on *The Tonight Show with Jay Leno*. At one point, Kermit appeared about to venture into sexist territory. Fortunately, Ms. lang warned him not to go there. Kermit gulped — and did not go there.[197]

• Because of the Jim Crow laws that prevented gospel singer Mahalia Jackson from eating in white-only restaurants or sleeping in white-only hotels, she bought a Cadillac for when she toured in the South. Her car had to be large enough for her to carry food in it — and to sleep in it.[198]

• Before the beginning of World War II, contralto Marian Anderson's reputation spread rapidly, and she was invited to sing in Germany, which was then ruled by Adolf Hitler. However, when the Germans discovered that Ms. Anderson was an African American, they withdrew the offer.[199]

• In 1931, jazz musician Louis Armstrong returned to his native New Orleans, where he appeared on a local radio show. Mr. Armstrong was forced to introduce himself on the show because the white announcer refused to announce a black musician.[200]

• During the Jim Crow days, Pierre Monteux tried to register at a hotel, but he was told that it was a hotel for colored people only. Mr. Monteux protested, "But I am colored — pink."[201]

49

Chapter 5: From Problem-Solving to Work

Problem-Solving

• While Emma Albani was performing Desdemona to Signor Tamagno's *Otello*, Signor Tamagno insisted that the stage contain three steps down which he would roll when he died after strangling Desdemona on a bed on a platform at the top of the stairs. Unfortunately, although the stage did have the three steps, it had no platform on which the bed could stand. Therefore, four men knelt on their hands and knees and supported the bed on which Ms. Albani, as Desdemona, was strangled.[202]

• Some members of Duke Ellington's band drank too much, coming to performances drunk and posing a problem for Mr. Ellington, who had to either stop their alcohol abuse or get rid of them. Mr. Ellington used to deal with the problem by setting an impossible tempo, and then having the drunken musician attempt to give a solo. After the drunken soloist had made a fool of himself, he would either decide to stay sober or he would quit. No more problem.[203]

• Bette Midler got her start in the gay club known as the Continental Baths, where she was extremely popular. When she first started singing at a "real" nightclub, Downstairs at the Upstairs, no one came. Therefore, the Divine Miss M placed an ad in *Screw* magazine to let her gay fans know that "Bette from the Baths" was performing "at the Downstairs." After the ad appeared, the nightclub was packed with her fans.[204]

• Lily Pons' voice was small, and she disliked curtains at the back of the stage, fearing that they would absorb too much of the sound of her voice. Instead of curtains, she wanted flats or screens at the back of the stage, as they would help her project her voice. At a concert in the south, no flats or screens were on hand, so she borrowed eight ping-pong tables from the YMCA, removed their legs, and used them instead.[205]

• Some opera singers sing *forte* when they should sing *piano* because they are afraid that they won't be heard over the orchestra. Conductor Herbert von Karajan once was faced with a singer who did this. He solved the problem by telling her, "If you sing *piano*, I'll have the orchestra play *piano* and everybody will hear you. If you sing *forte*, I'll have the orchestra play *forte* and you'll never be heard in the first row." [206]

• Richard the Lionheart composed music with his minstrel, Blondel de Nesles. According to legend, when Richard was being held captive — no one knew where — Blondel traveled the countryside, going from one castle to another, singing a song that he and Richard had composed together. One day, Blondel sang the song in a castle, and a musical reply came to him — it was Richard.[207]

• At the Metropolitan Opera was a retired baritone named Désiré Defrère who still worked there and was very resourceful in meeting a crisis. Once, a singer at the Met ran out of breath before reaching a high note. Noticing this, Mr. Defrère sang the note offstage, and few people if any in the audience noticed that the singer on the stage had had a problem.[208]

• Concert pianist André Watts, an African American, grew up in a tough neighborhood in Philadelphia, the City of Brotherly Love, where the Irish and the Italian and the African-American kids fought each other. André was in a few fights, but the fights stopped after he learned enough judo to protect himself.[209]

• Enrico Caruso once rented a floor in a hotel that had uncomfortable Louis XVI chairs. His wife didn't like the chairs, but Mr. Caruso pointed out that they had an advantage: They were so uncomfortable that visitors did not stay long.[210]

Prodigies

• Ludwig van Beethoven's friend Carl Czerny insisted that he listen to a child prodigy, Franz Liszt, although Beethoven hated child prodigies. At first, Beethoven glowered at his visitors, but he did pay attention as Liszt played a piece by Ries, and then he asked Liszt to play a fugue by Bach. Liszt played the "Fugue in C Minor" from *The Well-Tempered Clavier*. Beethoven then asked the young Liszt, "Can you transpose the fugue straightaway to another key?" Liszt did, and Beethoven smiled. Next Liszt played a piece of Beethoven's, and Beethoven kissed him on the forehead and said, "You are a lucky fellow, for you are going to make lots of other people happy and gratified. There is nothing better or more beautiful."[211]

• Wolfgang Amadeus Mozart was a child prodigy, and his father made him tour throughout Europe, exhibiting his gifts on the piano. While returning home to Austria, Mozart played for the border guards, who then allowed him and his family to cross the border without paying the duty on the presents that had been given to Mozart by appreciative listeners.[212]

Programs

• Early in his career, James W. Morrissey hired Russian pianist Anton Rubinstein to give a series of concerts in New York. Seeking something that would appeal to the public, Mr. Morrissey arranged for a program of light music by Johann Strauss. However, when Mr. Rubinstein saw the program shortly before he was scheduled to perform, he absolutely refused to go on stage, explaining that he was a serious artist and would be disgraced if he were ever to play such music. Fortunately, Mr. Morrissey was able to arrange a substitute program of suitable serious music.[213]

• Pianist Josef Hoffman traveled much, giving recitals around the world. At the beginning of one recital, he had forgotten what he was supposed to play, so he walked over to a woman seated in the first row and asked to see her program.[214]

Rehearsals

• Even as a young conductor, Arturo Toscanini felt strongly about his art. When he was scheduled to conduct his first concert in Turin, he first rehearsed the orchestra in the orchestra pit, but he also wanted to rehearse the orchestra on the stage because that was where the orchestra would be during the concert and he wanted to make sure the orchestra would sound right from that location. However, the manager of the theater felt that rehearsing on the stage was not necessary, so Maestro Toscanini said that he would not conduct without the rehearsal. When the time of the concert came, Maestro Toscanini was home in bed. The manager came looking for him, but Maestro Toscanini still refused to conduct. The concert was given at a later date — after Maestro Toscanini had rehearsed the orchestra on the stage.[215]

• Wilhelm Pitz, chorus master of the Philharmonica Choir, did not believe in wasting rehearsal time. If the conductor were late or otherwise absent, Mr. Pitz would himself rehearse the choir. When Sir William Walton was in the middle of conducting his *Belshazzar's Feast* for a recording, he needed to leave to listen to a playback of a section that he had just recorded. When he returned, he found Mr. Pitz at the conductor's podium, guiding the choir in the production of beautiful music. Sir William listened until Mr. Pitz noticed him and left the podium. Sir William climbed up to the podium, and then sadly addressed the choir: "Why can't you do it like that for me?"[216]

• Operatic tenor Leo Slezak was known for his practical jokes during rehearsals. During a dress rehearsal of *Tannhäuser*, several horses were brought on stage, and all of them proceeded to behave badly, filling the stage with dung. After the rehearsal, Mr. Slezak in a hurt voice told the conductor of the opera, Herr Hertz, a man vehemently opposed to his practical joking, "You see how unjust you are. You don't say a word to the horses, but if I had done it, there would be the usual complaint — Slezak is interfering with the rehearsal!"[217]

• The indefatigable Sir Henry Wood insisted on having an adequate number of rehearsals when he conducted. Arturo Toscanini once conducted Beethoven's Ninth Symphony in London, and very shortly thereafter Sir Henry decided to conduct the Ninth using the same orchestra and the same soloists that Toscanini had used. Sir Henry insisted on having five rehearsals, but the powers that be said that three would be enough — after all, Toscanini had had only three rehearsals. Sir Henry replied, "Really — perhaps *he* gets tired."[218]

• Soccer and Cup Final day are important in England. Once, the noted conductor Sir Thomas Beecham held a rehearsal on Cup Final day. The rehearsal had been going on for only a short time when a giant television was delivered to the rehearsal area. Sir Thomas then said, "Now, gentlemen, let's get down to the most important business of the day — watching the match."[219]

Revenge

• Perhaps the most famous of all operatic mishaps occurred in 1961 at the City Center in New York because stagehands got angry at a soprano who was temperamental. At the end of the opera *Tosca*, the soprano, playing the lead role, was to throw herself off the battlements of a castle — landing, of course, on soft padding in the orchestra pit out of sight of the audience. But for this performance, the stagehands substituted a trampoline for the usual soft padding, so that the soprano bounced back into the full view of the audience.[220]

• Maria Callas once behaved badly to fellow singer Leonne Mills, so Ms. Mills took revenge. She was singing Inez in *Il Trovatore*, and just before going on stage, she ate a large onion, and then sang her role directly into Ms. Callas' face.[221]

Songwriters

• As a famous singer, Nat King Cole was besieged by songwriters who wanted him to record their songs. He was once trapped in a men's room by a songwriter who showed him his manuscript. Mr. Cole told the songwriter, "Please! Not here!" On another occasion, his bus was pulled over by an Oklahoman deputy sheriff who gave him a song manuscript instead of a ticket.[222]

• Songwriter Sammy Cahn, who won Oscars for "Three Coins in the Fountain," "Call Me Irresponsible," "All the Way," and "High Hopes," was often asked, "What comes first — the music or the lyric?" He always answered, "The phone call." (Whenever he answers the phone, he says cheerfully, "Here I am!")[223]

Television

• On the old TV game show *Name That Tune*, the two contestants were a beautiful French woman and an American sailor. The orchestra played the tune they were to guess, "The Anniversary Waltz." The French woman guessed, "Oh, How Ve Danced on Ze Night Ve Vere Ved," but emcee Red Benson correctly pointed out that that wasn't the name of the song, but only a line from it. Then Mr. Benson turned to the sailor and gave him a hint to help him guess the title of "The Anniversary Waltz": "If you were married to this beautiful girl tonight, what would you be singing a year from now?" The sailor answered, "Rock-a-Bye-Baby."[224]

• In 1998, pop singer Madonna performed a dance that is sacred to the Hindus. The World Vaishnava Association believed that Madonna's performing the dance was a sacrilege, and it demanded an apology. Madonna refused to apologize. Instead, she asked, "If they're so pure, why are they watching TV?"[225]

• When Johnny Carson was playing "Stump the Band" on *The Tonight Show*, he called on a woman to participate. The woman was obviously pregnant, and when Mr. Carson asked her name, "You are ...," she replied, "Yes."[226]

Tempi

• Conductor Wilhelm Furtwängler took the various tempi of Wagner's *Ring* cycle quicker than the London Philharmonic Orchestra was used to, and this almost led to a triangle player not performing. In *Rheingold*, triangle player Charlie Turner had a long wait before he played, so he used to disappear into a nearby bar while keeping a close eye on the time so he could get back to the orchestra and play.

One night, the members of the orchestra were getting quite worried because Mr. Turner had still not made an appearance with only a few bars to go. Suddenly, they heard running footsteps. Just in time, the door to the orchestra pit opened and a hand reached out and struck the triangle, and then disappeared again. The next day, Mr. Turner had his stopwatch out, timing the faster-tempo music to make sure that he would arrive at the pit with time to spare.[227]

• Alexandra Danilova was getting ready to dance in *Cimarosiana* one night when a good-looking, well-dressed man said to her, "Good evening. What tempo will you be dancing tonight?" She replied, "I'm sorry. I don't talk to strangers, and I don't believe we've been introduced." While dancing on stage, she saw the man again — he was conducting the orchestra. Thomas Beecham, who was supposed to conduct, was ill, and so this man — Malcolm Sargent — had filled in for him. Ms. Danilova says that Mr. Sargent set a "perfect" tempo for her.[228]

• While Jimmy Stein and other members of the band were playing Latin American music in a restaurant, a waiter grabbed the maracas and started shaking them — out of tempo. Mr. Stein stopped playing and asked the waiter, "What do you think you're doing?" The waiter said that he always played the marimbas during Latin American music, but Mr. Stein told him, "Not with my instruments, you don't." As the waiter was leaving, Mr. Stein called after him, "I don't come into your kitchen and play with your bloody knives and forks, do I?"[229]

Travel

• After a long night of traveling, soprano Adelina Patti stopped at 5 a.m. for a few hours rest in Warsaw. Unfortunately, at 6 a.m. what sounded like a racket to the tired soprano broke out next door as someone began to play a piano. Outraged, Ms. Patti sent a servant to ask the noise-maker to stop playing the piano — at least until 8 a.m. The noise-maker stopped, and Ms. Patti's husband, the Marquise de Caux, sent his card to him in thanks. A moment later, the noise-maker himself appeared at Ms. Patti's door to ask politely about her. The famous soprano and her husband were shocked to learn that the noise-maker was the eminent pianist Hans von Bülow.[230]

• After soprano Marjorie Lawrence appeared as Brünnhilde in St. Louis, she left the theater in full costume and makeup because her train was scheduled to leave quickly. Unfortunately, even though she left the theater and went to the train station right away, the train pulled out just as she reached the station. Therefore, she was driven to the next train stop, where — still wearing her Brünnhilde makeup and costume — she boarded the wrong car. Walking through several cars until she reached her car, she startled the passengers, and one person called out, "It must be a holdup!"[231]

• During the early 20th century, dancer Anna Pavlova toured in Texas. There, her music director, Theodore Stier, found some of the dirtiest theaters it was his misfortune to conduct in. In one Texas dressing room, he discovered an empty ink bottle. One year later, he returned to the same theater and the same dressing room, and he discovered the same empty ink bottle. For the next two years, he returned to the same dressing room — each year, he found the same empty ink bottle.[232]

• Opera singer Leo Slezak did not like to share train compartments with strangers. He carried a sign saying "RESERVIERT" when he traveled by train and displayed it on the door after staking his claim on a compartment. Whenever the train was especially crowded, he used another sign: "HOSPITAL COMPARTMENT." With the use of the signs (and a few bribes to the train employees), he was able to travel in privacy.[233]

• Las Vegas hasn't always been famous. Bill Bailey, the brother of Pearl Bailey, once had a job in Las Vegas, but he failed to show up for opening night. While driving there, he had come to two signs in the road. One sign pointed to Las Vegas, Nevada; the other sign pointed to Las Vegas, New Mexico. Unfortunately, Mr. Bailey took the wrong road.[234]

• After a worldwide tour in which she spent 150 days at sea and visited Australia, the United States, and the Orient, Emma Calvé experienced eye trouble and went to see a doctor. He told her, "What do you expect? Of course your eyes are tired! You have seen more in the last few months than I have seen in all my seventy years!"[235]

• While sailing in the ship *Parakoola*, opera soprano Marjorie Lawrence practiced singing *Elektra*. Unfortunately, the sailors were not used to hearing opera. When Ms. Lawrence practiced *Elektra* for the first time, the sailors came running to her cabin to see what was wrong with her.[236]

• Pop singer Jewel — Jewel Kilcher — was raised in Alaska on her family's 800-acre homestead. Wherever she travels, she carries a container filled with earth from her family's homestead.[237]

War

• During World War I, Thomas Beecham wanted to conduct some operas by the German composer Richard Wagner; however, an English patriot who ran a newspaper felt that playing German music when England was at war with Germany was unpatriotic and so he demanded that Mr. Beecham either not conduct Wagnerian opera or face the wrath of the press. Fortunately, Mr. Beecham knew that the patriot had some very fine German paintings, and he offered not to conduct Wagner provided the patriot burn his German paintings in public. When Mr. Beecham made his proposal to the patriot, the patriot was silent for a time, and then smiled and said, "It is rather silly, isn't it?" Mr. Beecham was thereafter left to conduct Wagner in peace.[238]

• During World War II, while she was still very young, Maria Callas sang in front of an audience that included a German soldier from the army then occupying Greece. The German soldier was entranced by Maria's singing, and exclaimed to a woman sitting next to him, "What an artist! What a singer! That girl will be famous!" The woman then revealed that she was Evangelia Callas, Maria's mother, and the German soldier kissed her. She cried out, "Don't do that! You are the enemy!" The German soldier laughed, and then gave her another kiss, saying, "I can be enemy to no woman with a daughter like yours, Madam. I shall never forget you or her."[239]

• On December 30, 1862, during the Civil War, the Confederate and the Union forces camped near each other by Stone's River, which is located close to Murfreesboro, Tennessee. That night, the military bands of the two armies competed against each other, with the Confederate band playing patriotic songs of the South and the Union band playing patriotic songs of the North. Eventually, however, the Union band started playing "Home Sweet Home," and quickly the Confederate band joined in, so that both bands were playing the same song together.[240]

• When the Germans and Italians occupied Athens, Greece, during World War II, one of their rules required the Athenians to remain silent — even in their own homes. The Greeks enjoyed breaking this rule. Maria Callas, and then a teenager, used to sing the lead role of *Tosca* with windows and doors wide open, and across the rooftops the voice of an unknown man responded, singing the role of Mario.[241]

Work

• After Schuyler Chapin became general manager of the New York Metropolitan Opera, he acquired the problems that all opera managers acquire. On the very first Saturday morning of his very first season as general manager, he was faced with three problems. First, Mirella Freni let him know that she would not honor her contract because of "*your* Internal Revenue Service." Second, Tito Gobbi cancelled as Iago because of illness. Third, conductor Erich Leinsdorf demanded another *Die Walkure* Wotan. Faced with all these problems within the space of 20 minutes, Mr. Chapin closed his door, walked over to his window, and asked himself, "You *wanted* this job?"[242]

• One of soprano Rita Hunter's early voice teachers was Eva Turner. Unfortunately, when the two parted company, Ms. Turner told Ms. Hunter, "My dear, you will never make a singer — you will have to scrub floors for a living." This turned out not to be true, although Ms. Hunter did continue to scrub her own floors. In fact, when a contract to sing for the Metropolitan Opera arrived in the mail, Ms. Hunter was scrubbing a floor. And after the Queen made her a Commander of the British Empire because of her singing, Ms. Hunter told a reporter that being made a CBE had made little difference in her life because "they still let me scrub the floors."[243]

• Puppeteer Shari Lewis of "Lamp Chop" fame declined to hire assistants unless they had been trained in music. Therefore, during interviews, she asked first, "Did you ever study a musical instrument?" Why? Through experience, she had learned that people with a solid music education know that they can accomplish whatever goal they have set even when they begin without knowing anything. Her assistants have included an opera singer, a jazz singer, and a guitarist. [244]

• Gregor Piatigorsky, a virtuoso cellist, once asked conductor Pierre Monteux for permission to conduct "The Star-Bangled Banner," which Maestro Monteux granted. After "The Star-Spangled Banner" had been played, Maestro Monteux asked Mr. Piatigorsky how the conducting had gone. "It was easy," Mr. Piatigorsky said. Maestro Monteux replied, "Don't tell anybody."[245]

• When the Archduke Rudolph was appointed Archbishop of Olmütz, Ludwig van Beethoven wanted to write some music for the celebration. He started to write his *Mass in D*, but he became so involved in the music, and the music grew so great in conception, that the celebration had been over for two years by the time Beethoven completed the work.[246]

• Blind Lemon Jefferson, a blues singer and guitarist, was born blind. As a young man, he moved to Dallas, Texas, where he found it difficult to get work. However, because he was a big, strong man who weighed 250 pounds, he was able to get a job as a wrestler. Crowds of people were willing to pay to see him because a blind wrestler was unusual.[247]

• Sometimes, people don't realize how difficult making music can be. After hearing that Bill Worland was a professional musician, a woman told him, "Sitting playing the piano for three or four hours, I don't call that hard work — it's easy." Mr. Worland replied, "Yes, it's easy. It only takes a lifetime to learn how to do it, and do it well."[248]

• On June 20, 1994, Aretha Franklin gave a memorable performance at the White House Rose Garden for then-President Bill Clinton and other guests. In fact, while singing "Brand New Me," she performed so hard that while crossing the stage she lost a shoe.[249]

• When George Gershwin was told that the woman he loved had married another man, he said, "I'd feel terrible about this if I weren't so busy."[250]

Appendix A: Bibliography

Abdul, Raoul. *Famous Black Entertainers of Today*. New York: Dodd, Mead & Company, 1974.

Albani, Emma. *Forty Years of Song*. New York: Arno Press. 1977.

Alda, Frances. *Men, Women, and Tenors*. Boston, MA: Houghton Mifflin Company, 1937.

Atkins, Harold and Archie Newman, compilers. *Beecham Stories*. Great Britain: Futura Publications Limited, 1978.

Ayre, Leslie. *The Wit of Music*. Boston, MA: Crescendo Publishing Company, 1969.

Barber, David W. *Bach, Beethoven, and the Boys*. Toronto, Canada: Sound and Vision, 1996.

Barber, David W. *Getting a Handel on Messiah*. Toronto, Canada: Sound and Vision, 1994.

Beach, Scott. *Musicdotes*. Berkeley, CA: Ten Speed Press, 1977.

Beecham, Thomas. *A Mingled Chime*. New York: Da Capo Press, 1976.

Bing, Sir Rudolf. *5000 Nights at the Opera*. Garden City, NY: Doubleday and Company, Inc., 1972.

Blackwood, Alan. *The Performing World of the Singer*. Morristown, N.J.: Silver Burdett Company, 1981.

Bonvicini, Candido. *The Tenor's Son: My Days With Pavarotti*. New York: St. Martin's Press, 1992.

Borge, Victor, and Robert Sherman. *My Favorite Comedies in Music*. New York: Franklin Watts, 1980.

Borge, Victor, and Robert Sherman. *My Favorite Intermissions*. Garden City, NY: Doubleday and Co., Inc., 1971.

Boxer, Tim. *The Jewish Celebrity Hall of Fame*. New York: Shapolsky Publishers, 1987.

Boyden, John, collector. *Stick to the Music: Scores of Orchestral Tales*. London: Souvenir Press, 1992.

Bracken, Peg. *The I Hate to Housekeep Book*. New York: Harcourt, Brace and World, Inc., 1962.

Breckenridge, W.K. *Anecdotes of Great Musicians*. New York: Pageant Press, Inc., 1955.

Breslin, Herbert H., editor. *The Tenors*. New York: Macmillan Publishing Co., Inc., 1974.

Broadwater, Andrea. *Marian Anderson: Singer and Humanitarian.* Berkeley Heights, NJ: Enslow Publications, Inc., 2000.

Bronski, Michael, consulting editor. *Outstanding Lives: Profiles of Lesbians and Gay Men.* Foreword by Jewelle L. Gomez; Christa Brelin and Michael J. Tyrkus, editors. Detroit, MI: Visible Ink Press, 1997.

Callas, Evangelia. *My Daughter Maria Callas.* New York: Fleet Publishing Corporation, 1960.

Calvé, Emma. *My Life.* Translated by Rosamond Gilder. New York. Arno Press, 1977.

Cardus, Neville, editor. *Kathleen Ferrier: A Memoir.* London: Hamish Hamilton, Ltd., 1954.

Caruso, Dorothy. *Enrico Caruso: His Life and Death.* New York: Simon and Schuster, Inc., 1945.

Chapin, Schuyler. *Sopranos, Mezzos, Tenors, Bassos, and Other Friends.* New York: Crown Publishers, Inc., 1995.

Chapman, Graham. *Graham Crackers.* Compiled by Jim Yoakum. Franklin Lakes, NJ: Career Press, Inc., 1997.

Chotzinoff, Samuel. *Toscanini: An Intimate Portrait.* New York: Alfred A. Knopf, 1956.

Cole, Maria. *Nat King Cole: An Intimate Biography.* New York: William Morrow and Company, Inc., 1971.

Cott, Ted. *The Victor Book of Musical Fun.* New York: Simon and Schuster, Inc., 1945.

Cowan, Lore and Maurice. *The Wit of the Jews.* Nashville, TN: Aurora Publishers, Limited, 1970.

Cruz, Barbara C. *Rubén Blades: Salsa Singer and Social Activist.* Springfield, NJ: Enslow Publications, Inc., 1997.

Czerny, Carl. *On the Proper Performance of All Beethoven's Piano Works.* Edited by Paul Badura-Skoda. USA: Universal Edition, 1970.

Danilova, Alexandra. *Choura: The Memoirs of Alexandra Danilova.* New York: Alfred A. Knopf, 1986.

Domingo, Plácido. *My First Forty Years.* New York: Alfred A Knopf, 1983.

Douglas, Nigel. *Legendary Voices.* London: Andre Deutsch, Limited, 1992.

Douglas, Nigel. *More Legendary Voices.* London: Andre Deutsch, Limited, 1994.

Drake, James A, and Kristin Beall Ludecke, editors. *Lily Pons: A Centennial Portrait.* Portland, OR: Amadeus Press, 1999.

Drucker, Hal, and Sid Lerner. *From the Desk Of.* Photographs by Sing-Si Schwartz. San Diego, CA: Harcourt Brace Jovanovich, Publishers, 1989.

Ewen, David. *Famous Modern Conductors*. New York: Dodd, Mead & Company, 1967.

Ewen, David, complier. *Listen to the Mocking Words*. New York: Arco Publishing Co., 1945.

Farrar, Geraldine. *Geraldine Farrar: The Story of an American Singer*. Boston, MA, and New York: Houghton Mifflin Company, 1916.

Farrar, Geraldine. *Such Sweet Compulsion*. New York: The Greystone Press, 1938.

Feather, Leonard, and Jack Tracy. *Laughter from the Hip: The Lighter Side of Jazz*. New York: Da Capo Press, Inc., 1979.

Finck, Henry T. *Musical Laughs*. New York: Funk & Wagnalls Company, 1924.

Ford, Michael Thomas. *It's Not Mean If It's True*. Los Angeles, CA: Alyson Books, 2000.

Foxx, Redd, and Norma Miller. *The Redd Foxx Encyclopedia of Black Humor*. Pasadena, CA: Ward Ritchie Press, 1977.

Garden, Mary, and Louis Biancolli. *Mary Garden's Story*. New York: Simon and Schuster, Inc., 1951.

Garrett, Leslie. *Notes from a Small Soprano*. London: Hodder and Stoughton, 2000.

Gelfand, Ravina, and Letha Patterson. *They Wouldn't Quit: Stories of Handicapped People*. Minneapolis, MN: Lerner Publications Company, 1962.

Goodnough, David. *Pablo Casals: Cellist for the World*. Springfield, NJ: Enslow Publications, Inc., 1997.

Greenberg, Keith Elliot. *Rap*. Minneapolis, MN: Lerner Publications Company, 1988.

Grenfell, Joyce. *Joyce Grenfell Requests the Pleasure*. London: Macdonald Futura Publishers, Ltd., 1976.

Groover, David L., and Cecil C. Conner, Jr. *Skeletons from the Opera Closet*. New York: St. Martin's Press, 1986.

Guttmacher, Peter. *Legendary Comedies*. New York: MetroBooks, 1996.

Hacker, Carlotta. *Great African Americans in Jazz*. New York: Crabtree Publishing Company, 1997.

Haggin, B.H. *Conversations With Toscanini*. Garden City, NY: Doubleday & Co., Inc., 1959.

Hecht, Andrew. *Hollywood Merry-Go-Round*. New York: Grosset and Dunlap, Publishers, 1947.

Hewlett-Davies, Barry, editor and compiler. *A Night at the Opera*. New York: St. Martin's Press, 1980.

Hintz, Martin. *Farewell, John Barleycorn: Prohibition in the United States*. Minneapolis, MN: Lerner Publications Company, 1996.

Holloway, Stanley. *Wiv a Little Bit O' Luck.* As told to Dick Richards. New York: Stein and Day, Publishers, 1967.

Humphrey, Laning, compiler. *The Humor of Music and Other Oddities in the Art.* Boston, MA: Crescendo Publishing Company, 1971.

Hunter, Rita. *Wait Till the Sun Shines, Nellie.* London: Hamish Hamilton Ltd., 1986.

Hunter, Shaun. *Visual and Performing Artists.* New York: Crabtree Publishing Company, 1999.

Hurok, S. *S. Hurok Presents: A Memoir of the Dance World.* New York: Hermitage House, 1953.

Jackson, Jesse. *Make a Joyful Noise unto the Lord! The Life of Mahalia Jackson, Queen of Gospel Singers.* New York: Thomas Y. Crowell Company, 1974.

Josephson, Judith Pinkerton. *Nikki Giovanni: Poet of the People.* Berkeley Heights, NJ: Enslow Publications, Inc., 2000.

Kallen, Stuart A. *Great Composers.* San Diego, CA: Lucent Books, 2000.

Katella-Cofrancesco, Kathy. *Children's Causes.* Brookfield, CT: Twenty-First Century Books, 1998.

Katella-Cofrancesco, Kathy. *Economic Causes.* Brookfield, CT: Twenty-First Century Books. 1998.

Kaufmann, Helen L. *Anecdotes of Music and Musicians.* New York: Grosset & Dunlap, Publishers, 1960.

Kent, Zachary. *The Civil War: "A House Divided."* Hillside, NJ: Enslow Publications, Inc., 1994.

Kistler, Darci. *Ballerina: My Story.* With Alicia Kistler. New York: Pocket Books, Inc., 1993.

Kliment, Bud. *Billie Holiday.* New York: Chelsea House Publishers, 1990.

Knapp, Ron. *American Legends of Rock.* Springfield, NJ: Enslow Publications, Inc., 1996.

Laffey, Bruce. *Beatrice Lillie: The Funniest Woman in the World.* New York: Wynwood Press, 1989.

Lauw, Louisa. *Fourteen Years with Adelina Patti.* [s.l.] La Scala Autographs, 1977.

Lawrence, Marjorie. *Interrupted Melody: The Story of My Life.* New York: Appleton-Century-Crofts, Inc., 1949.

Lester, Julius. *The Blues Singers: Ten Who Rocked the World.* New York: Hyperion Books for Children, 2001.

Lehmann, Lotte. *Midway in My Song: The Autobiography of Lotte Lehmann.* Freeport, NY: Books for Libraries Press, 1970.

Levant, Oscar. *A Smattering of Ignorance.* New York: Doubleday, Doran, and Co., 1940.

Linkletter, Art. *I Wish I'd Said That! My Favorite Ad-Libs of All Time*. Garden City, NY: Doubleday & Co., Inc., 1968.

Linkletter, Art. *Oops! Or, Life's Awful Moments*. Garden City, NY: Doubleday & Company, Inc., 1967.

Long, Rod. *Belly Laughs*. Renton, WI: Talion Publishing, 1999.

Malone, Mary. *Will Rogers: Cowboy Philosopher*. Springfield, NJ: Enslow Publications, Inc., 1996.

Mandelbaum, Yitta Halberstam. *Holy Brother: Inspiring Stories and Enchanted Tales About Rabbi Shlomo Carlebach*. Northvale, NJ: Jason Aronson Inc., 1997.

Mapleson, Colonel J.H. *The Mapleson Memoirs: The Career of an Operatic Impresario, 1858-1888*. Edited by Harold Rosenthal. New York: Appleton-Century, 1966.

Markova, Alicia. *Markova Remembers*. Boston, MA: Little, Brown and Company, 1986.

Marques, Herón. *Latin Sensations*. Minneapolis, MN: Lerner Publications Company, 2001.

Matthews, Denis. *In Pursuit of Music*. London: Victor Gollancz, Ltd., 1966.

McArthur, Edwin. *Flagstad: A Personal Memoir*. New York: Alfred A. Knopf, 1965.

Meek, Harold. *Horn and Conductor: Reminiscences of a Practitioner with a Few Words of Advice*. Rochester, NY: University of Rochester Press, 1997.

Midler, Bette. *A View from a Broad*. New York: Simon and Schuster, Inc. 1980.

Miller, Norma. *Swinging' at the Savoy*. With Evette Jensen. Philadelphia, PA: Temple University Press, 1996.

Moore, Carmen. *Somebody's Angel Child: The Story of Bessie Smith*. New York: Dell Publishing Co., 1969.

Morgan, Henry. *Here's Morgan!* New York: Barricade Books, Inc., 1994.

Morrissey, James W. *Noted Men and Women*. New York: The Klebold Press, 1910.

Mostel, Kate, and Madeline Gilford. *170 Years of Show Business*. With Jack Gilford and Zero Mostel. New York: Random House, 1978.

Mour, Stanley I. *American Jazz Musicians*. Springfield, NJ: Enslow Publications, Inc., 1998.

Music Educators National Conference, editors. *The Gifts of Music*. Reston, VA: Music Educators National Conference, 1994.

Nicholson, Frank Ernest. *Favorite Jokes of Famous People*. New York: E.P. Dutton & Co., Inc., 1928.

Old, Wendie C. *Duke Ellington: Giant of Jazz*. Springfield, NJ: Enslow Publications, Inc., 1996.

Old, Wendie C. *Louis Armstrong: King of Jazz*. Springfield, NJ: Enslow Publications, Inc., 1998.

Opera Magazine Ltd. *Sopranos in Opera: Profiles of Fifteen Great Sopranos*. London: Opera Magazine Ltd., 2002.

Orgill, Roxane. *Shout, Sister, Shout!* New York: Margaret K. McElderry Books, 2001.

Pellowski, Michael J. *Baseball's Funniest People*. New York: Sterling Publishing Co., 1997.

Pollack, Barbara, and Charles Humphrey Woodford. *Dance is a Moment: A Portrait of José Limón in Words and Pictures*. Pennington, NJ: Princeton Book Company, Publishers, 1993.

Procter-Gregg, Humphrey. *Beecham Remembered*. London: Gerald Duckworth & Company Limited, 1976.

Ravitch, Diane, editor. *The American Reader: Words That Moved a Nation*. New York: HarperCollins Publishers, 1990.

Rediger, Pat. *Great African Americans in Music*. New York: Crabtree Publishing Company, 1996.

Reely, Trey. *Move Over Mr. Holland*. Paragould, AR: [s.n.], 1999.

Robinson, Simon. *A Year With Rudolf Nureyev*. With Derek Robinson. London: Robert Hale, Limited, 1997.

Rogers, Francis. *Some Famous Singers of the 19th Century*. New York: Arno Press, 1977.

Russell, Anna. *I'm Not Making This Up, You Know: The Autobiography of the Queen of Musical Parody*. New York: The Continuum Publishing Company, 1985.

Savage, Richard Temple. *A Voice from the Pit*. Newton Abbot; North Pomfret, VT: David & Charles, 1988.

Schafer, Kermit. *All Time Great Bloopers*. New York: Avenel Books, 1973.

Schafer, Kermit. *Kermit Schafer's Blunderful World of Bloopers*. New York: Bounty Books, 1973.

Scherer, Barrymore Laurence. *Bravo! A Guide to Opera for the Perplexed*. New York: Dutton, 1996.

Seroff, Victor. *Renata Tebaldi: The Woman and the Diva*. Freeport, NY: Books for Libraries Press, 1970.

Sheafer, Silvia Anne. *Aretha Franklin: Motown Superstar*. Springfield, NJ: Enslow Publications, Inc., 1996.

Sherman, Russell. *Piano Pieces*. New York: Farrar, Straus, and Giroux, 1996.

Slezak, Leo. *Song of Motley*. New York: Arno Press, 1977.

Slezak, Walter. *What Time's the Next Swan?* Garden City, NY: Doubleday and Co., Inc., 1962.

Stier, Theodore. *With Pavlova Around the World*. London: Hurst & Blackett, Ltd., 1927.

Story, Rosalyn M. *And So I Sing: African-American Divas of Opera and Concert*. New York: Warner Books, 1990.

Surge, Frank. *Singers of the Blues*. Minneapolis, MN: Lerner Publications Company, 1969.

Vickers, Hugh. *Even Greater Operatic Disasters*. New York: St. Martin's Press, 1982.

Vickers, Hugh. *Great Operatic Disasters*. Introduction by Sir Peter Ustinov. New York: St. Martin's Press, Inc., 1979.

Wagner, Alan. *Prima Donnas and Other Wild Beasts*. Larchmont, NY: Argonaut Books, 1961.

Williams, Kenneth. *Acid Drops*. London: J. M. Dent & Sons, Ltd., 1980.

Willson, Meredith. *And There I Stood With My Piccolo*. Westport, CT: Greenwood Press, Publishers, 1948.

Worland, Bill. *"Fumble Four Bars In."* London: Minerva Press, 1996.

Wright, David K. *Paul Robeson: Actor, Singer, Political Activist*. Berkeley Heights, NJ: Enslow Publications, Inc., 1998.

Zolotow, Maurice. *No People Like Show People*. New York: Random House, 1951.

Zymet, Cathy Alter. *Ricky Martin*. Philadelphia, PA: Chelsea House Publishers, 2001.

Appendix B: About the Author

It was a dark and stormy night. Suddenly a cry rang out, and on a hot summer night in 1954, Josephine, wife of Carl Bruce, gave birth to a boy — me. Unfortunately, this young married couple allowed Reuben Saturday, Josephine's brother, to name their first-born. Reuben, aka "The Joker," decided that Bruce was a nice name, so he decided to name me Bruce Bruce. I have gone by my middle name — David — ever since.

Being named Bruce David Bruce hasn't been all bad. Bank tellers remember me very quickly, so I don't often have to show an ID. It can be fun in charades, also. When I was a counselor as a teenager at Camp Echoing Hills in Warsaw, Ohio, a fellow counselor gave the signs for "sounds like" and "two words," then she pointed to a bruise on her leg twice. Bruise Bruise? Oh yeah, Bruce Bruce is the answer!

Uncle Reuben, by the way, gave me a haircut when I was in kindergarten. He cut my hair short and shaved a small bald spot on the back of my head. My mother wouldn't let me go to school until the bald spot grew out again.

Of all my brothers and sisters (six in all), I am the only transplant to Athens, Ohio. I was born in Newark, Ohio, and have lived all around Southeastern Ohio. However, I moved to Athens to go to Ohio University and have never left.

At Ohio U, I never could make up my mind whether to major in English or Philosophy, so I got a bachelor's degree with a double major in both areas, then I added a Master of Arts degree in English and a Master of Arts degree in Philosophy. Yes, I have my MAMA degree.

Currently, and for a long time to come (I eat fruits and veggies), I am spending my retirement writing books such as *Nadia Comaneci: Perfect 10*, *The Funniest People in Comedy*, *Homer's* Iliad: *A Retelling in Prose*, and *William Shakespeare's* Hamlet: *A Retelling in Prose*.

By the way, my sister Brenda Kennedy writes romances such as *A New Beginning* and *Shattered Dreams*.

Appendix C: Some Books by David Bruce

Anecdote Collections

250 Anecdotes About Opera

250 Anecdotes About Religion

250 Anecdotes About Religion: Volume 2

250 Music Anecdotes

Be a Work of Art: 250 Anecdotes and Stories

The Coolest People in Art: 250 Anecdotes

The Coolest People in the Arts: 250 Anecdotes

The Coolest People in Books: 250 Anecdotes

The Coolest People in Comedy: 250 Anecdotes

Create, Then Take a Break: 250 Anecdotes

Don't Fear the Reaper: 250 Anecdotes

The Funniest People in Art: 250 Anecdotes

The Funniest People in Books: 250 Anecdotes

The Funniest People in Books, Volume 2: 250 Anecdotes

The Funniest People in Books, Volume 3: 250 Anecdotes

The Funniest People in Comedy: 250 Anecdotes

The Funniest People in Dance: 250 Anecdotes

The Funniest People in Families: 250 Anecdotes

The Funniest People in Families, Volume 2: 250 Anecdotes

The Funniest People in Families, Volume 3: 250 Anecdotes

The Funniest People in Families, Volume 4: 250 Anecdotes

The Funniest People in Families, Volume 5: 250 Anecdotes

The Funniest People in Families, Volume 6: 250 Anecdotes

The Funniest People in Movies: 250 Anecdotes

The Funniest People in Music: 250 Anecdotes

The Funniest People in Music, Volume 2: 250 Anecdotes

The Funniest People in Music, Volume 3: 250 Anecdotes

The Funniest People in Neighborhoods: 250 Anecdotes

The Funniest People in Relationships: 250 Anecdotes

The Funniest People in Sports: 250 Anecdotes

The Funniest People in Sports, Volume 2: 250 Anecdotes

The Funniest People in Television and Radio: 250 Anecdotes

The Funniest People in Theater: 250 Anecdotes

The Funniest People Who Live Life: 250 Anecdotes
The Funniest People Who Live Life, Volume 2: 250 Anecdotes
The Kindest People Who Do Good Deeds, Volume 1: 250 Anecdotes
The Kindest People Who Do Good Deeds, Volume 2: 250 Anecdotes
Maximum Cool: 250 Anecdotes
The Most Interesting People in Movies: 250 Anecdotes
The Most Interesting People in Politics and History: 250 Anecdotes
The Most Interesting People in Politics and History, Volume 2: 250 Anecdotes
The Most Interesting People in Politics and History, Volume 3: 250 Anecdotes
The Most Interesting People in Religion: 250 Anecdotes
The Most Interesting People in Sports: 250 Anecdotes
The Most Interesting People Who Live Life: 250 Anecdotes
The Most Interesting People Who Live Life, Volume 2: 250 Anecdotes
Reality is Fabulous: 250 Anecdotes and Stories
Resist Psychic Death: 250 Anecdotes
Seize the Day: 250 Anecdotes and Stories

---

[1]Source: Stanley I. Mour, *American Jazz Musicians*, pp. 35-36.

[2]Source: David K. Wright, *Paul Robeson: Actor, Singer, Political Activist*, p. 94.

[3]Source: David Goodnough, *Pablo Casals: Cellist for the World*, pp. 65-66, 97.

[4]Source: Wendie C. Old, *Louis Armstrong: King of Jazz*, p. 99.

[5]Source: Lore and Maurice Cowan, *The Wit of the Jews*, p. 62.

[6]Source: Leslie Ayre, *The Wit of Music*, p. 21.

[7]Source: Laning Humphrey, compiler, *The Humor of Music and Other Oddities in the Art*, p. 9.

[8]Source: Humphrey Procter-Gregg, *Beecham Remembered*, p. 188.

[9]Source: Herón Marques, *Latin Sensations*, p. 39.

[10]Source: Theodore Stier, *With Pavlova Around the World*, pp. 113-114.

[11]Source: Edwin McArthur, *Flagstad: A Personal Memoir*, p. 14.

[12]Source: Joyce Grenfell, *Joyce Grenfell Requests the Pleasure*, p. 208.

[13]Source: Hugh Vickers, *Even Greater Operatic Disasters*, p. 67.

[14]Source: W.K. Breckenridge, *Anecdotes of Great Musicians*, p. 7.

[15]Source: Barry Hewlett-Davies, *A Night at the Opera*, pp. 16-17.

[16]Source: David Ewen, *Listen to the Mocking Words*, p. 65.

[17]Source: Barrymore Laurence Scherer, *Bravo! A Guide to Opera for the Perplexed*, p. 23.

[18]Source: Nigel Douglas, *Legendary Voices*, pp. 169-170.

[19]Source: David Ewen, *Famous Modern Conductors*, p. 15.

[20]Source: Alan Wagner, *Prima Donnas and Other Wild Beasts*, pp. 9-10.

[21]Source: Sir Rudolf Bing, *5000 Nights at the Opera*, p. 28.

[22]Source: Scott Beach, *Musicdotes*, p. 58.

[23]Source: Victor Borge and Robert Sherman, *My Favorite Intermissions*, p. 64.

[24]Source: Opera Magazine Ltd., *Sopranos in Opera: Profiles of Fifteen Great Sopranos*, p. 29.

[25]Source: Schuyler Chapin, *Sopranos, Mezzos, Tenors, Bassos, and Other Friends*, p. 207.

[26]Source: Nigel Douglas, *More Legendary Voices*, p. 110.

[27]Source: Edwin McArthur, *Flagstad: A Personal Memoir*, p. 30.

[28]Source: Nigel Douglas, *More Legendary Voices*, p. 140.

[29]Source: Pat Rediger, *Great African Americans in Music*, p. 18.

[30]Source: Diane Ravitch, *The American Reader*, p. 280.

[31]Source: Leslie Garrett, *Notes from a Small Soprano*, p. 245.

[32]Source: Victor Borge and Robert Sherman, *My Favorite Comedies in Music*, p. 131.

[33]Source: Mary Garden and Louis Biancolli, *Mary Garden's Story*, pp. 25ff.

[34]Source: Shaun Hunter, *Visual and Performing Artists*, pp. 37-38.

[35]Source: Denis Matthews, *In Pursuit of Music*, p. 120.

[36]Source: Thomas Beecham, *A Mingled Chime*, pp. 295-296.

[37]Source: Humphrey Procter-Gregg, *Beecham Remembered*, p. 189.

[38]Source: Geraldine Farrar, *Geraldine Farrar: The Story of an American Singer*, p. 5.

[39]Source: Joyce Grenfell, *Joyce Grenfell Requests the Pleasure*, p. 26.

[40]Source: Walter Slezak, *What Time's the Next Swan?*, pp. 30-31.

[41]Source: Frank Surge, *Singers of the Blues*, p. 40.

[42]Source: Peg Bracken, *The I Hate to Housekeep Book*, p. 114.

[43]Source: Denis Matthews, *In Pursuit of Music*, p. 145.

[44]Source: Opera Magazine Ltd., *Sopranos in Opera: Profiles of Fifteen Great Sopranos*, p. 51.

[45]Source: David Ewen, *Famous Modern Conductors*, p. 94.

[46]Source: Lotte Lehmann, *Midway in My Song*, pp. 2-3.

[47]Source: Bruce Laffey, *Beatrice Lillie*, p. 17.

[48]Source: Alan Blackwood, *The Performing World of the Singer*, p. 66.

[49]Source: Lotte Lehmann, *Midway in My Song*, p. 24.

[50]Source: Kermit Schafer, *Kermit Schafer's Blunderful World of Bloopers*, p. 311.

[51]Source: Julius Lester, *The Blues Singers: Ten Who Rocked the World*, p. 40.

[52]Source: Shaun Hunter, *Visual and Performing Artists*, p. 19.

[53]Source: Mary Malone, *Will Rogers: Cowboy Philosopher*, p. 54.

[54]Source: Maurice Zolotow, *No People Like Show People*, p. 164.

[55]Source: Carl Czerny, *On the Proper Performance of All Beethoven's Piano Works*, p. 4.

[56]Source: Alexandra Danilova, *Choura*, p. 127.

[57]Source: David W. Barber, *Bach, Beethoven, and the Boys*, p. 60.

[58]Source: David L. Groover and Cecil C. Conner, Jr., *Skeletons from the Opera Closet*, p. 231.

[59]Source: Meredith Willson, *And There I Stood With My Piccolo*, pp. 98-101.

[60]Source: John Boyden, collector, *Stick to the Music: Scores of Orchestral Tales*, pp. 85-86.

[61]Source: B.H. Haggin, *Conversations With Toscanini*, pp. 27, 30.

[62]Source: Samuel Chotzinoff, *Toscanini: An Intimate Portrait*, pp. 36-37.

[63]Source: Henry T. Finck, *Musical Laughs*, p. 105.

[64]Source: Ted Cott, *The Victor Book of Musical Fun*, p. 45.

[65]Source: Harold Meek, *Horn and Conductor*, p. 2.

[66]Source: David Goodnough, *Pablo Casals: Cellist for the World*, p. 54.

[67]Source: Barbara Pollack and Charles Humphrey Woodford, *Dance is a Moment*, p. 68.

[68]Source: S. Hurok, *S. Hurok Presents*, pp. 81-82.

[69]Source: Leslie Garrett, *Notes from a Small Soprano*, pp. 107, 143-144.

[70]Source: Frances Alda, *Men, Women, and Tenors*, pp. 14-15.

[71]Source: Mary Garden and Louis Biancolli, *Mary Garden's Story*, p. 173.

[72]Source: Maurice Zolotow, *No People Like Show People*, pp. 292-293.

[73]Source: Victor Seroff, *Renata Tebaldi: The Woman and the Diva*, p. 156.

[74]Source: Kenneth Williams, *Acid Drops*, p. 22.

[75]Source: Julius Lester, *The Blues Singers: Ten Who Rocked the World*, p. 20.

[76]Source: Alicia Markova, *Markova Remembers*, p. 110.

[77]Source: Darci Kistler, *Ballerina: My Story*, p. 41.

[78]Source: Yitta Halberstam Mandelbaum, *Holy Brother*, pp. 30-31.

[79]Source: Harold Atkins and Archie Newman, *Beecham Stories*, p. 41.

[80]Source: Simon Robinson, *A Year With Rudolf Nureyev*, p. 45.

[81]Source: Keith Elliot Greenberg, *Rap*, pp. 24-25.

[82]Source: Stuart A. Kallen, *Great Composers*, p. 50.

[83]Source: Music Educators National Conference, editors, *The Gifts of Music*, p. 36.

[84]Source: Trey Reely, *Move Over Mr. Holland*, p. 134.

[85]Source: David W. Barber, *Getting a Handel on Messiah*, p. 26.

[86]Source: Anna Russell, *I'm Not Making This Up, You Know*, p. 60.

[87]Source: Peter Guttmacher, *Legendary Comedies*, p. 72.

[88]Source: Kathy Katella-Cofrancesco, *Children's Causes*, pp. 43, 45.

[89]Source: Geraldine Farrar, *Such Sweet Compulsion*, p. 33.

[90]Source: David L. Groover and Cecil C. Conner, Jr., *Skeletons from the Opera Closet*, p. 219-220.

[91]Source: Stanley Holloway, *Wiv a Little Bit O' Luck*, p. 158.

[92]Source: Carlotta Hacker, *Great African Americans in Jazz*, p. 35.

[93]Source: Ron Knapp, *American Legends of Rock*, p. 95.

[94]Source: Stuart A. Kallen, *Great Composers*, p. 68.

[95]Source: Michael Thomas Ford, *It's Not Mean If It's True*, pp. 18-19.

[96]Source: Yitta Halberstam Mandelbaum, *Holy Brother*, pp. 161-162.

[97]Source: Nigel Douglas, *Legendary Voices*, pp. 49, 51.

[98]Source: Tim Boxer, *The Jewish Celebrity Hall of Fame*, p. 219.

[99]Source: David W. Barber, *Getting a Handel on Messiah*, pp. 48-49.

[100]Source: Kathy Lynn Gray, "'60s pop singer makes fans feel like it was only yesterday." *The Columbus Dispatch*. August 18, 2000. Page C3.

[101]Source: an A&E *Biography* episode featuring the Beatles.

[102]Source: Alan Wagner, *Prima Donnas and Other Wild Beasts*, p. 110.

[103]Source: Oscar Levant, *A Smattering of Ignorance*, p. 170.

[104]Source: Tim Boxer, *The Jewish Celebrity Hall of Fame*, pp. 75-76.

[105]Source: Michael Bronski, consulting editor, *Outstanding Lives*, p. 114.

[106]Source: Emma Calvé, *My Life*, p. 50.

[107]Source: Bud Kliment, *Billie Holiday*, pp. 74-75.

[108]Source: Peg Bracken, *The I Hate to Housekeep Book*, pp. 20-21.

[109]Source: Victor Seroff, *Renata Tebaldi: The Woman and the Diva*, pp. 144-145.

[110]Source: Samuel Chotzinoff, *Toscanini: An Intimate Portrait*, p. 13.

[111]Source: Helen L. Kaufmann, *Anecdotes of Music and Musicians*, pp. 66-67.

[112]Source: Carmen Moore, *Somebody's Angel Child: The Story of Bessie Smith*, pp. 73-74.

[113]Source: Alicia Markova, *Markova Remembers*, p. 86.

[114]Source: Wendie C. Old, *Louis Armstrong: King of Jazz*, p. 42.

[115]Source: Graham Chapman, *Graham Crackers*, pp. 151-152.

[116]Source: Candido Bonvicini, *The Tenor's Son: My Days With Pavarotti*, pp. 138-139.

[117]Source: Simon Robinson, *A Year With Rudolf Nureyev*, p. 45.

[118]Source: Bette Midler, *A View from a Broad*, p. 39.

[119]Source: Michael Thomas Ford, *It's Not Mean If It's True*, pp. 88-89.

[120]Source: Ron Knapp, *American Legends of Rock*, pp. 46, 49.

[121]Source: Emma Albani, *Forty Years of Song*, p. 144.

[122]Source: Michael J. Pellowski, *Baseball's Funniest People*, p. 27.

[123]Source: Rita Hunter, *Wait Till the Sun Shines, Nellie*, p. 153.

[124]Source: Stanley Holloway, *Wiv a Little Bit O' Luck*, p. 124.

[125]Source: Louisa Lauw, *Fourteen Years with Adelina Patti*, pp. 50-51.

[126]Source: Frank Ernest Nicholson, *Favorite Jokes of Famous People*, pp. 21-22.

[127]Source: Carmen Moore, *Somebody's Angel Child: The Story of Bessie Smith*, pp. 91-92.

[128]Source: Francis Rogers, *Some Famous Singers of the 19th Century*, p. 103.

[129]Source: Bette Midler, *A View from a Broad*, p. 132.

[130]Source: Keith Elliot Greenberg, *Rap*, p. 9.

[131]Source: Geraldine Farrar, *Such Sweet Compulsion*, p. 132.

[132]Source: Barrymore Laurence Scherer, *Bravo! A Guide to Opera for the Perplexed*, p. 197.

[133]Source: Trey Reely, *Move Over Mr. Holland*, p. 117.

[134]Source: Scott Beach, *Musicdotes*, p. 63.

[135]Source: Graham Chapman, *Graham Crackers*, pp. 155-156.

[136]Source: Plácido Domingo, *My First Forty Years*, pp. 91-92.

[137]Source: Colonel J. H. Mapleson, *The Mapleson Memoirs*, pp. 204-205.

[138]Source: James W. Morrissey, *Noted Men and Women*, pp. 51-54.

[139]Source: David Ewen, *Listen to the Mocking Words*, pp. 41-42.

[140]Source: Rosalyn M. Story, *And So I Sing: African-American Divas of Opera and Concert*, pp. 40-41.

[141]Source: Herón Marques, *Latin Sensations*, pp. 74-75.

[142]Source: Barbara C. Cruz, *Rubén Blades: Salsa Singer and Social Activist*, pp. 38, 68-69.

[143]Source: Geraldine Farrar, *Geraldine Farrar: The Story of an American Singer*, pp. 45-46.

[144]Source: Cathy Alter Zymet, *Ricky Martin*, p. 48.

[145]Source: Meredith Willson, *And There I Stood With My Piccolo*, pp. 101-103.

[146]Source: Andrew Hecht, *Hollywood Merry-Go-Round*, p. 139.

[147]Source: Barry Hewlett-Davies, *A Night at the Opera*, p. 26.

[148]Source: Plácido Domingo, *My First Forty Years*, pp. 3-4.

[149]Source: Redd Foxx and Norma Miller, *The Redd Foxx Encyclopedia of Black Humor*, p. 158.

[150]Source: Neville Cardus, editor, *Kathleen Ferrier: A Memoir*, p. 77.

[151]Source: James A. Drake and Kristin Beall Ludecke, editors, *Lily Pons: A Centennial Portrait*, pp. 182-183.

[152]Source: Art Linkletter, *Oops!*, pp. 62-64.

[153]Source: Herbert H. Breslin, editor, *The Tenors*, pp. 104-105.

[154]Source: Bruce Laffey, *Beatrice Lillie*, pp. 248-249.

[155]Source: Kermit Schafer, *All Time Great Bloopers*, p. 14.

[156]Source: Art Linkletter, *I Wish I'd Said That!*, p. 15.

[157]Source: Colonel J. H. Mapleson, *The Mapleson Memoirs*, pp. 182-183.

[158]Source: David W. Barber, *Bach, Beethoven, and the Boys*, p. 11.

[159]Source: Art Linkletter, *I Wish I'd Said That!*, p. 20.

[160]Source: Candido Bonvicini, *The Tenor's Son: My Days With Pavarotti*, pp. 55-56.

[161]Source: Oscar Levant, *A Smattering of Ignorance*, pp. 30-31.

[162]Source: Neville Cardus, editor, *Kathleen Ferrier: A Memoir*, p. 63.

[163]Source: Russell Sherman, *Piano Pieces*, p. 61.

[164]Source: Peter Guttmacher, *Legendary Comedies*, p. 37.

[165]Source: Wendie C. Old, *Duke Ellington: Giant of Jazz*, p. 71.

[166]Source: Frances Alda, *Men, Women, and Tenors*, pp. 167-168.

[167]Source: Laning Humphrey, compiler, *The Humor of Music and Other Oddities in the Art*, p. 23.

[168]Source: Helen L. Kaufmann, *Anecdotes of Music and Musicians*, pp. 35-36.

[169]Source: Carlotta Hacker, *Great African Americans in Jazz*, p. 15.

[170]Source: Pat Rediger, *Great African Americans in Music*, p. 14.

[171]Source: Dorothy Caruso, *Enrico Caruso: His Life and Death*, p. 66.

[172]Source: Bartcop. 26 June 2003 <www.bartcop.com>.

[173]Source: Ravina Gelfand and Letha Patterson, *They Wouldn't Quit: Stories of Handicapped People*, pp. 12-15.

[174]Source: Rod Long, *Belly Laughs*, pp. 102-103.

[175]Source: Hal Drucker and Sid Lerner, *From the Desk Of*, p. 68.

[176]Source: W.K. Breckenridge, *Anecdotes of Great Musicians*, p. 13.

[177]Source: Russell Sherman, *Piano Pieces*, p. 36

[178]Source: Barbara Pollack and Charles Humphrey Woodford, *Dance is a Moment*, p. 67

[179]Source: Andrew Hecht, *Hollywood Merry-Go-Round*, p. 140.

[180]Source: Victor Borge and Robert Sherman, *My Favorite Comedies in Music*, pp. 131-132.

[181]Source: Martin Hintz, *Farewell, John Barleycorn: Prohibition in the United States*, pp. 53, 55.

[182]Source: Anna Russell, *I'm Not Making This Up, You Know*, p. 138.

[183]Source: Leo Slezak, *Song of Motley*, pp. 291-292.

[184]Source: Hugh Vickers, *Even Greater Operatic Disasters*, p. 51.

[185]Source: Rosalyn M. Story, *And So I Sing: African-American Divas of Opera and Concert*, p. 146.

[186]Source: Andrea Broadwater, *Marian Anderson: Singer and Humanitarian*, p. 67.

[187]Source: Leonard Feather and Jack Tracy, *Laughter from the Hip: The Lighter Side of Jazz*, p. 99.

[188]Source: Jesse Jackson, *Make a Joyful Noise unto the Lord! The Life of Mahalia Jackson, Queen of Gospel Singers*, p. 118.

[189]Source: Maria Cole, *Nat King Cole: An Intimate Biography*, p. 78.

[190]Source: David K. Wright, *Paul Robeson: Actor, Singer, Political Activist*, pp. 115-116.

[191]Source: Kate Mostel and Madeline Gilford, *170 Years of Show Business*, p. 95.

[192]Source: Francis Rogers, *Some Famous Singers of the 19th Century*, p. 53.

[193]Source: Bud Kliment, *Billie Holiday*, p. 62.

[194]Source: Henry Morgan, *Here's Morgan!*, p. 18.

[195]Source: Ernie Smith, "Preface" to Norma Miller, *Swingin' at the Savoy*, p. xxxii.

[196]Source: Leonard Feather and Jack Tracy, *Laughter from the Hip: The Lighter Side of Jazz*, p. 94.

[197]Source: Michael Bronski, consulting editor, *Outstanding Lives*, p. 243.

[198]Source: Jesse Jackson, *Make a Joyful Noise unto the Lord! The Life of Mahalia Jackson, Queen of Gospel Singers*, p. 97.

[199]Source: Andrea Broadwater, *Marian Anderson: Singer and Humanitarian*, pp. 54-55.

[200]Source: Stanley I. Mour, *American Jazz Musicians*, p. 24.

[201]Source: Kenneth Williams, *Acid Drops*, p. 109.

[202]Source: Emma Albani, *Forty Years of Song*, pp. 222-223.

[203]Source: Wendie C. Old, *Duke Ellington: Giant of Jazz*, pp. 65-66.

[204]Source: Roxane Orgill, *Shout, Sister, Shout!*, p. 97.

[205]Source: James A. Drake and Kristin Beall Ludecke, editors, *Lily Pons: A Centennial Portrait*, p. 104.

[206]Source: Herbert H. Breslin, editor, *The Tenors*, p. 192.

[207]Source: Alan Blackwood, *The Performing World of the Singer*, pp. 4-5.

[208]Source: Sir Rudolf Bing, *5000 Nights at the Opera*, p. 141.

[209]Source: Raoul Abdul, *Famous Black Entertainers of Today*, p. 142.

[210]Source: Dorothy Caruso, *Enrico Caruso: His Life and Death*, pp. 259-260.

[211]Source: Carl Czerny, *On the Proper Performance of All Beethoven's Piano Works*, p. 7.

[212]Source: Victor Borge and Robert Sherman, *My Favorite Intermissions*, p. 37.

[213]Source: James W. Morrissey, *Noted Men and Women*, pp. 29ff.

[214]Source: Henry T. Finck, *Musical Laughs*, p. 46.

[215]Source: B.H. Haggin, *Conversations With Toscanini*, p. 104.

[216]Source: John Boyden, collector, *Stick to the Music: Scores of Orchestral Tales*, pp. 108-109.

[217]Source: Leo Slezak, *Song of Motley*, pp. 99-100.

[218]Source: Leslie Ayre, *The Wit of Music*, pp. 14-15.

[219]Source: Harold Atkins and Archie Newman, *Beecham Stories*, p. 72.

[220]Source: Hugh Vickers, *Great Operatic Disasters*, p. 12.

[221]Source: Richard Temple Savage, *A Voice from the Pit*, p. 142.

[222]Source: Maria Cole, *Nat King Cole: An Intimate Biography*, p. 29.

[223]Source: Hal Drucker and Sid Lerner, *From the Desk Of*, p. 8.

[224]Source: Kermit Schafer, *Kermit Schafer's Blunderful World of Bloopers*, p. 114.

[225]Source: Roxane Orgill, *Shout, Sister, Shout!*, p. 112.

[226]Source: Kermit Schafer, *All Time Great Bloopers*, p. 42.

[227]Source: Richard Temple Savage, *A Voice from the Pit*, p. 54.

[228]Source: Alexandra Danilova, *Choura*, p. 105.

[229]Source: Bill Worland, *"Fumble Four Bars In,"* p. 147.

[230]Source: Louisa Lauw, *Fourteen Years with Adelina Patti*, p. 60.

[231]Source: Marjorie Lawrence, *Interrupted Melody: The Story of My Life*, p. 161.

[232]Source: Theodore Stier, *With Pavlova Around the World*, pp. 105-106.

[233]Source: Walter Slezak, *What Time's the Next Swan?*, p. 21.

[234]Source: Norma Miller, *Swinging' at the Savoy*, pp. 204-205.

[235]Source: Emma Calvé, *My Life*, pp. 211-212.

[236]Source: Marjorie Lawrence, *Interrupted Melody: The Story of My Life*, p. 247.

[237]Source: Kathy Katella-Cofrancesco, *Economic Causes*, p. 26.

[238]Source: Thomas Beecham, *A Mingled Chime*, p. 270.

[239]Source: Evangelia Callas, *My Daughter Maria Callas*, p. 66.

[240]Source: Zachary Kent, *The Civil War: "A House Divided,"* p. 36.

[241]Source: Evangelia Callas, *My Daughter Maria Callas*, p. 56.

[242]Source: Schuyler Chapin, *Sopranos, Mezzos, Tenors, Bassos, and Other Friends*, p. 180.

[243]Source: Rita Hunter, *Wait Till the Sun Shines, Nellie*, p. 70.

[244]Source: Music Educators National Conference, editors, *The Gifts of Music*, p. 103.

[245]Source: Harold Meek, *Horn and Conductor*, p. 26.

[246]Source: Ted Cott, *The Victor Book of Musical Fun*, p. 41.

[247]Source: Frank Surge, *Singers of the Blues*, p. 21.

[248]Source: Bill Worland, *"Fumble Four Bars In,"* p. 200.

[249]Source: Silvia Anne Sheafer, *Aretha Franklin: Motown Superstar*, pp. 7, 10.

[250]Source: Lore and Maurice Cowan, *The Wit of the Jews*, p. 86.

9 798215 681633